THE) STARTED HERE!

Mark Llewellin
Foreword by Jimmie Chinn

P & D Riley

First published 2000

P & D Riley
12 Bridgeway East,
Cheshire,
WA7 6LD,
England

E-mail: pdriley@lineone.net

ISBN: 1 874712 47 6

British Library Cataloguing in Publication Data
A catalogue Record for this book is available from the British Library

Printed and bound in England

Introduction and acknowledgments

In 1995 a friend of mine invited to me to join him in visiting the 'Oldham Coliseum' to see the premiere of a play called "Sylvia's Wedding". I had heard of the 'Coliseum' though I had never actually been there, indeed I'd never even been to Oldham!

The play was by a new friend of mine called Jimmie Chinn - at that time I had no idea that he was an Oldhamer - and it starred Lynette McMorrough, Norman Rossington, Frederick Pyne and Sally Ann Matthews. The 'Coliseum' was a revelation to me - friendly staff, intimate auditorium and a cracking cast. From then on I began to become a regular attender.

A year on and I went to see the pantomime "Dick Whittington" at Nottingham Playhouse starring Kenneth Alan Taylor (one of his many retirement seasons!) and we got talking in the bar after the show. Kenneth had just been appointed Chief Executive at the 'Coliseum' and I told him of my desire to work there.

My story then moves on to October 1997 when I saw the post of Marketing and Press Manager advertised in 'The Stage' - I applied and got the job. Jimmie Chinn was staying at my house at the time and so the story sort of comes full circle!

When Peter Riley asked me to consider writing a book on the 'Coliseum' I immediately agreed - over the past five years or so I have followed so many people by falling under the spell of this little theatre. It has almost a unique history and has launched the careers of so many household names and faces over the years that it surely deserves perhaps a little more respect than it gets these days. It is therefore my privilege to attempt to document what makes the 'rep' so special.

Someone once said that to copy from one book is plagiarism but to copy from lots of books is research - well, I gladly acknowledge the help of so many people with this project - all the 'Coliseum' staff past and present particularly Sue Evans who catalogued the whole archive with me, Jane Doxey, David Rustidge and of course, Kenneth Alan Taylor, the staff of the Oldham Chronicle, all those actors and writers who contributed and gave of their time, Jimmie Chinn, those who took all the fabulous photographs, and Peter Riley for being so encouraging.

I have read just about every programme note written between 1920 and 2000 and it is largely from these that I have chosen to tell the tale - at least here I have found people's own words and after all, this is not really the story of bricks but of people. I hope I have told it like it was! I must also apologise to those who read hoping to see their name in print - I have listed many of the actors who have trodden the boards here over the years however, space has allowed me to list only a cross-section of names that may be familiar to you - over two thousand actors have appeared at the 'Coliseum' over the last sixty years or so and it would have been impossible to list them all. Incidentally, where actors have changed their names I have used the name by which they are known today.

Finally, I hope you enjoy learning more about your local theatre!

Mark Llewellin

About the author

Mark Llewellin trained in performing arts at Wakefield College. After graduating he took up a post with Mountview Theatre School in London and subsequently worked in marketing for British Airways, British Telecom and London Transport. In 1997 he was appointed as Marketing and Press Manager for Oldham Coliseum Theatre, being promoted to Marketing Director in 2000. He is also a director of the marketing consultancy, Volcano Associates.

Mark is a seasoned performer having appeared on stage on many occasions, written and directed his own pantomimes and created and performed the role of Uncle Silas on BBC GMR for over a year.

Oldham town centre in 1897

Foreword
By Jimmie Chinn

I first went to the 'Coliseum' back in 1953. It was known simply as the 'rep' in those days. I must have been thirteen and the play was called "Busman's Honeymoon", a thriller in which the murder weapon turned out to be a hanging pot-plant! The actors included Ronald Magill, Tony Tanner, Keith Marsh and Madeleine Newbury .... Oh, and Gillian Charles who later married 'rep' actor Bernard Cribbins, now a friend of mine, and they remain married to this day. The 'producer' of the play (he'd be called the director now) was Harry Lomax who, along with Eric Longworth, was in charge of the artistic policy for most of the fifties. I can still remember vividly that first visit - it changed my life in fact - the look, the feel, even the smell of that cosy little theatre. From that evening on I was hooked - theatre was in my blood.

As Mark Llewellin points out in this concise and wholly captivating history of the 'Coliseum' and its people, the 'rep' was a club back then and you had to be a member in order to buy a ticket (one and sixpence for juniors as I recall) and I always carried my membership card next to my heart! Once a week, on a Tuesday, a different play every time, I would catch the 59 bus from Middleton where I lived, get off at the corner of Fairbottom Street, enjoy beans on toast and a glass of Vimto in the Kings Café opposite the theatre where most of the actors would be drinking coffee and smoking cigarettes (oh how I longed to be one of them!), then over the road to my favourite seat in the stalls - centre aisle third row from the back - a Lyons Maid choc-ice in the interval or, when the nights were chilly, a cup of hot Oxo and a biscuit served on a tray in your seat. For a lad with his head in the clouds all this was the very height of sophistication and pleasure. And why, you may well ask, do I remember it all so clearly after almost half a century? That's what Mr Llewellin's book does for you.

Here, in this temple of drama, tucked away in a quiet Oldham cul-de-sac, I was introduced to the works of Shakespeare, Shaw, Wilde, Coward, Rattigan, Priestley, Ibsen, Moliere, Arthur Miller, Tennessee Williams and hundreds more: Agatha Christie of course and an endless stream of Lancashire comedies by writers such as Harold Brighouse, Walter Greenwood and Jack Popplewell. This was where I first saw "Macbeth", "The Dream", "King Lear", "A View From The Bridge", "Look Back In Anger" and "Murder At Quay Cottage"! "What?" I hear you cry - but I remember them all - good plays, great plays, bad plays - they were all wonderful to an impressionable youth like me.

Of course, if anyone had asked me then how it was all done, how all those actors, directors, designers and technicians managed, week after week, to create such theatrical magic, I would not have been able to answer. I still can't. Nor, I suspect, could most of the actors who worked at the 'Coliseum' in its weekly rep days - they were much too busy even to think about it: performing one play in the evenings (plus two matinees!), rehearsing another play during the day, and very often learning a third in bed at nights! Now tell me, how does any human being do that? Or does it, I often wonder, mean that actors are a breed apart from us mere mortals? As one of the characters in the film "Shakespeare In Love" so aptly puts it - "It's all a mystery!".

Only very occasionally were we the audience aware that things backstage were not running as smoothly as they should : the 'Asian Flu' epidemic which swept through Oldham in the mid-fifties, when people were dropping like flies and the cast of Priestley's "The Glass Cage" (whatever happened to that play?) had to be changed so often during its week's run that the actors had to go on most nights and read their parts from the script : a certain Tuesday matinee when only about a dozen of us had managed to battle through a snow storm and the theatre was so cold we were issued with blankets to keep us from freezing to death : the production of a Moliere comedy which had to be performed in modern dress on a Seventeenth century set because the hired costumes and wigs had failed to turn up! But whatever the crisis and in true theatrical tradition the battle call was always the same - "The show must go on!"

It is this rallying cry that seems to echo again and again as Mark Llewellin takes us on a fascinating journey to trace the history of the 'Coliseum' back to when it was built in the late 1880's (as a circus would you believe!), stopping off at each decade, up until the present day. And what a wealth of wonderful stories his painstaking research has uncovered. He writes about the building itself of course, and explains in detail how and why it has had to change over the years, but as he states in his introduction, this little book is mainly about, and dedicated to, the hundreds of people, both on stage and off, who like himself have fallen under the spell of this unique playhouse and worked tirelessly and unselfishly, often against the most impossible odds, to keep its doors open and its loyal and loving audiences entertained.

Maybe, in this new century, one of the greatest mysteries of all is how, in an age of stay at home push button entertainment, an age when so many regional repertory theatres have long since disappeared, the 'Coliseum' has managed to survive it all. And not only has it survived but, as I write this foreword, is as successful as it has ever been - still producing work of the highest quality - drama, comedy, musicals, and its annual traditional pantomime to warm and appreciative audiences still hungry for an evening of 'live' theatre at a very reasonable price!

Not only does Mark Llewellin try to solve this mystery but would also be the first to acknowledge that the theatre's present success is due mainly to the dedicated staff and management who work tirelessly to ensure that this remarkable, intimate and friendly little playhouse continues to flourish.

Chapter 1: All change!
Before 1885

Between 1801 and 1851 Oldham's population had increased from 12,000 to 53,000 fuelled by the growth of the cotton industry. With sheep farming in Saddleworth and mills in Oldham, the area provided the necessary catalyst for a major regional boom resulting in Lancashire cloth being exported all over the world. By 1861 the population was up again to 72,000, 1871 and it was 82,000 and by 1881 it was an incredible 111,000 - almost a ten fold increase in just eighty years.

Nationally, the latter half of the nineteenth century heralded cheaper food, rising wages and a general increase in confidence amongst working people - Oldhamers were no exception. It was also a period of development and improvement in conditions - the 'Co-operative' movement arrived in Oldham during 1851, Oldham Infirmary opened in 1872, gas supplies were reaching ordinary homes for the first time from around 1875, horse drawn trams were introduced from 1880, and perhaps most importantly, factories and mills began to allow workers a regular seasonal holiday from the 1870's.

As Oldham's population expanded and people found they had a mix of both time and money in their pockets for the first time, so the town attracted entrepreneurs from the leisure industries - train excursions became popular, as did such pastimes as smoking, drinking, the 'Temperance' movement and sport. It was a period that saw the foundation of great organisations - 'Oldham Cricket Club' in 1852, 'Oldham Rugby Club' in 1876, the 'Football Association' in 1863, the doomed 'Oldham Racecourse' in 1864, 'Oldham Musical Society' in 1886 and the 'Lyceum School of Music' in 1892. Oldham also got its first real taste of theatre!

To be historically accurate, Oldham's very first theatre was the 'New' which had opened in 1810 in Eagle Street near the bottom of West Street. Owned by one William Ryley, who seemed to have had rather a chequered history, the 'New' operated on and off for just over thirty years however, it was twenty years or so before Oldham got its second chance to become a town of theatregoers.

With the opening of the 'People's Hall of Varieties' in Rock Street in the 1860's the town got its very own music hall visited by such stars of the day as Vesta Tilley and in 1883, Dan Leno, who won a clog dancing championship there. In 1848 the 'Theatre Royal' opened on Horsedge Street, in 1868 the three thousand seater 'Adelphi Theatre' opened on Union Street, the 'Empire Theatre' on Waterloo Street in 1897 and in 1908, the 'Palace Theatre' and the 'Grand Theatre' both opened on Union Street. The only theatre surviving in the town today however, is the 'Coliseum' which opened originally in 1885 in Henshaw Street under the name 'Colosseum'.

Right: Dan Leno

A local pub showing an advertisement for the Colosseum and the Empire

The exterior of The Lyceum as it looks today

The Grand Theatre

8

Chapter 2: Join the Circus!
1885 - 1903

In 1880 two great showmen, P.T. Barnum and James A. Bailey joined forces to mount the very first 'Barnum and Bailey' circus spectacular under the banner "The Greatest Show on Earth". Three years later "Buffalo Bill" Cody began staging his legendary circus shows, which included frantic simulated "Indian attacks" and "feats of shooting". By the mid-1880's both shows were visiting England and proving a sensation - Queen Victoria was a regular attender although she was reported as being, "Quite fearful of the Indians who came so close". The popularity and publicity surrounding these productions spawned many copies, some good and some not so good.

In 1885 a man by the name of J.W. Myers visited Oldham and decided it would make the perfect home for his "Grand American Circus". He chose a site in Henshaw Street and contracted local builder and Mayor's son, Thomas Whittaker to build the round wooden building, which was to be named the 'Colosseum'. Unfortunately, when the time came to settle the bill Myers admitted that he had been unable to raise the necessary cash and a bitter court battle ensued. Myers claimed that the building was inadequate citing the fact the one of his lions had died whilst being kept at the property but the court was having none of it and in one of those wonderful twists of fate, Whittaker found himself the owner of a brand new circus.

It is perhaps a tribute to Whittaker's business acumen that he decided to keep the property and make a go of this new venture. The 'Colosseum' opened around the middle of 1885 with a "Chinese Fair"

Buffalo Bill Cody came to Oldham in 1895

followed by an equestrian season, the main attraction of which was a re-enactment of "Dick Turpin's Ride To York". Eventually Whittaker expanded the programme to include firstly, music hall acts and later, plays. Just as everything seemed to be going well for Thomas Whittaker the council announced its intention to build a Market Hall in Henshaw Street, slap bang on the site of the theatre (The market's name 'Tommyfield' commemorates the fact that it used to be a field belonging to Thomas Whittaker). By now, show business must have taken a hold of Whittaker because rather than sell up he hatched an elaborate

Thomas Whittaker

plan to find a new site and move his theatre plank by plank to its new home.

At that time Fairbottom Street led to the disused 'Holebottom Colliery' (there were several working mines in Oldham town centre up until the early 1880's) and to one side of it was the popular 'Theatre Royal'.

10

Whittaker decided that this would be a suitable site for his new look theatre and purchased part of the derelict mine - the in-filled reservoir to be precise! The plan caused much excitement in the town with the Oldham Chronicle reporting, "The great show of the future of Oldham will undoubtedly be the Colosseum. Right in the centre of Yorkshire Street and just conveniently enough off the thoroughfare to insure that peace and quietness - without which the Muses never feel altogether at home - Mr Whittaker has reared a Colosseum which the Romans of old would have been proud to hand down to posterity as a memorial of their skill and handiwork." Some unkind souls have noted that Yorkshire Street can still be rather like Rome at its height!

During 1887 the 'Colosseum' was indeed moved piece by piece to Fairbottom Street but Whittaker decided to improve upon the old facilities and add some new features to his theatre - for a variety of reasons.

As the theatre was built entirely of wood Whittaker sought to satisfy public health and safety concerns by installing exit doors with specially designed steel bars, which operated by pressure from inside and allowed full evacuation in two minutes - the forerunner of our modern emergency exit doors. He also offered a prize for the local Fire Brigade if they could set light to scrap ends of timber used in the construction - they couldn't and he took full use of the publicity to rename the theatre, 'The Colosseum - The Safe Theatre'. He installed gas lighting, footlights, a scene dock where cloths could be painted, an auditorium floor that could be raised to the level of the stage for public dancing, an air-conditioning system capable of providing cold, hot or perfumed air, and enough seating for three thousand people.

His investment was rewarded when the new theatre opened on June 10th 1887 with "Culeen's Royal Jubilee Circus". It was the very day that Queen Victoria celebrated fifty years on the throne and the theatre was honoured by being allowed to display her coat of arms over the stage. The Oldham Evening Chronicle reported, "The centre seats of the dress circle, upholstered in Utrecht velvet, rise gradually from the front, so that those behind can not only see over the heads of their male neighbours, but over the tallest feminine headgear that fashion can devise....the pit occupies the main body of the building right up to the orchestra, and is surrounded by a promenade, a screened bar being located in the middle. When this bar is in full swing it will be one of the attractions of the evening, the want of which now curtails the pleasure of local places of amusement."

Whittaker continued to manage his theatre until 1903 when he decided to sell up and concentrate on his building firm, the sale was to mark another radical change for the 'Colosseum'.

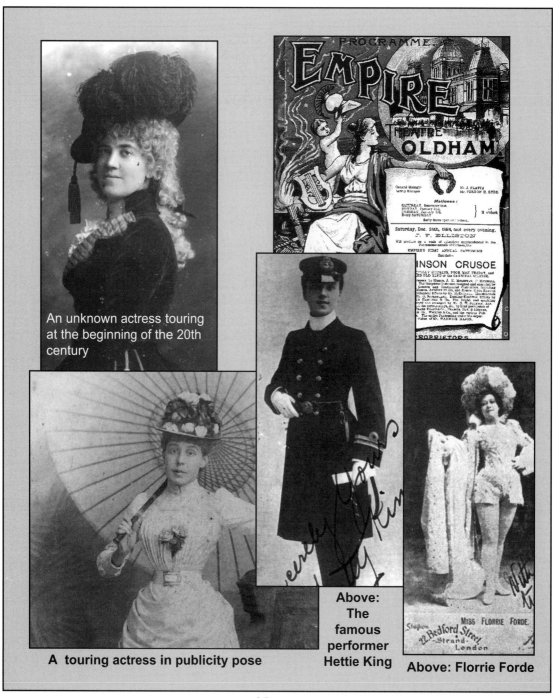

An unknown actress touring at the beginning of the 20th century

A touring actress in publicity pose

Above: The famous performer Hettie King

Above: Florrie Forde

Chapter 3: All change - again!
1903 - 1932

In February 1903 Thomas Whittaker ended his long association with the 'Colosseum' by selling it to one Joseph Ball for £4,000. The two men completed the deal it is said, as they travelled down Rochdale Road on a steam tram!

It turned out that Ball was acting on behalf of Peter Yates, owner of 'Yates' Wine Lodges', and that Ball and a friend called Ashton Heywood were to serve as lessees (they later expanded their empire to include the 'Gaiety Theatre'). Ball had run his own steeplejack business in Oldham for some time and become something of a local legend having dabbled with many ill-fated projects such as turning Chadderton Hall into a tropical zoo!

Under Ball and Heywood the 'Colosseum' offered the cheapest theatre seats in the town with those seats nearest the stage unusually being available at the lowest prices. An ever-changing programme offered visiting music hall, pantomime and circus. In 1906 Joseph Ball died, the same year that the council opened the Market Hall they had built in Henshaw Street - twenty years since the old 'Colosseum' had to be moved to make way for it!

The next few years were tough and the theatre provided a temporary home for touring companies producing opera, variety and pantomime. A number of later to be famous names appeared notably "Casey's Court Circus" starring Charlie Chaplin, and Stan Laurel in 'The Sleeping Beauty'. Despite all their best efforts however, black clouds were looming for the theatre largely due to the popularity of moving pictures.

Above left: Performer Harry Tate
Above right: A scene from a tour of
the play 'Beauty and the Barge'
Far Right: A young Charlie Chaplin.
Centre: Dora Levis, a touring actress
in a scene from 'Our Boys'.
Bottom right: A poster for the 1928
pantomime 'Cinderella'
Bottom: Charlie Chaplin in a theatre
scene from 'A Ticklish Job'

Again Oldham moved with the times and the opening of 'Brown's Picture Palace' in 1908 heralded a whole string of new movie theatres which included 'Dreamland' at Mumps, the 'Popular', the 'Palladium', and in 1911, the 'Kings' right opposite the 'Colosseum' in Fairbottom Street. In 1912 the owners decided they could no longer compete with the new cinemas and so silent films were shown alongside live acts and the building got another stay of execution.

With the 'Colosseum' and the 'Kings', tiny Fairbottom Street was a busy place at night and the queues would start forming on both sides of the street from about 7pm each evening with street traders walking the queues offering such wares as sweets, fruit and song books of the day.

In 1918 the 'Colosseum' was sold again, this time to 'Dobie's Electric Cinemas' who, along with the 'Royal Canadian Pictures Company', already owned a number of Oldham venues including the 'Emerald Hall' on Bartlam Place at the rear of the 'Colosseum'. The new owners continued with much the same format as the previous ones had done - jugglers and speciality acts appearing between films! On Sundays the auditorium was used for political meetings, lectures and demonstrations - Lloyd George, Ramsay Macdonald and Duff Cooper are amongst the famous orators to have addressed 'Colosseum' audiences.

By 1927 when "The Jazz Singer" was released as the first "talkie", a large number of theatres were being converted to full cinemas but the 'Colosseum' managed to hold on with its peculiar live and cinematic mix for another four years. In 1931 the 'Colosseum Super Talkie Theatre', as it was now known, got another new owner in the shape of William Cedric Bailey. Bailey converted the theatre to a full working cinema, shortened the depth of the auditorium and gave the interior a more modern feel. His idea was to show national releases plus his own home-made 'shorts' on such subjects as "Oldham Athletic Players at Watersheddings", "Boxing at Royton" and "Sporting Champions of the World".

What happened to Bailey and his plans isn't clear, however, we do know that under his ownership the cinema lasted but a few months and towards the end of 1931 a public auction was held at which such items as scenery, costumes and stage effects were disposed of. By the beginning of 1932 the 'Colosseum' was closed and left to fall into decay for some seven long years.

Above left: Major star Norman Evans pictured out of costume, and above right in his popular flat cap character.
Left: Owen Nares and Doris Keane in a scene from 'Romance'
Below: A poster from a 1908 performance at the Colosseum

COLOSSEUM
THEATRE, OLDHAM.

General Manager: WM. EASTWOOD.

THIS WEEK ONLY!
What the OLDHAM PRESS say about

The Nihilist

A magnificent production.
A drama of high-class merit.
Well worth a visit.
Not one portion of incident lacking.
So excellent are Mr. Walter Bentley's elocutionary powers that he has been engaged to lecture at many of our Universities.
Received with unmistakeable approval.
The play held the audience from start to finish.
There is some excellent fun.

Chapter 4: They call it progress!
1932-1938

The rise of the cinema did much to alter the make-up of Oldham's entertainment scene and to put a very large nail in the coffin of local theatre. Just like the 'Colosseum' many other theatres were converted into cinemas - The 'Adelphi' changed its name to the 'Victory' in 1920 (subsequent years saw life as a casino and then a "Continental Cinema"), the 'Empire' began showing films in 1911, the 'Palace' became the 'Odeon' in 1935, the 'Grand' became the 'Gaumont' in 1936 (subsequent years have seen it serve as a bowling alley and any number of night clubs), and the 'Theatre Royal' limped on as a theatre for many years, opening and closing several times, only to finally shut its doors in 1955 and be demolished in 1967.

The wheel of fortune continues to turn of course, and even the cinemas had their day and now, night clubs and pubs are the chief form of amusement in Oldham with the 'Kings Cinema', 'Victory' and the 'Gaumont' all having been converted to clubs. Today, there is talk of building a new cinema complex and a new theatre in Oldham town centre....they'll be bringing back the trams next!

With the closing of the 'Grand' in 1936 Oldham, which had only thirty years before boasted so many theatres, was left devoid of any real professional theatre or theatre company. This fact outraged at least one local actor and long time theatregoer called Joe Holroyd and he decided to set up a group to do something to remedy this sad situation.

The Victory Cinema today

Holroyd advertised for people who felt the same way as he did to join him at a committee meeting, which was held at the home of local teacher Phyllis Bennett. The turn out was very healthy and a local writer, Armitage Owen, agreed to pay for the hire of Greenacres Co-operative Hall where the little group could hold a full public meeting and at which they could sign up members.

Out of that gathering, the 'Oldham Playgoers' Club' was born and they campaigned to see the return of proper theatre to the town. The management of the 'Theatre Royal' seized on this demand and, with the support of the club, let the theatre to the 'Lawrence Williamson Company' who pledged to stage a varied programme of comedies and dramas. Unfortunately, this enterprise failed and despite some heated protests by the club's members, the 'Theatre Royal' reverted to a variety house.

For a while the club took up a temporary home at 'Billington's Dancing Academy' where they staged classical evenings, recitals and it is recorded, evenings of "Shakespearean strolling players". By 1937 the club had some ninety members and an ever-growing desire to see its aims achieved.

Back in 1844 a group of Owenites (followers of Robert Owen) had built a hall on Horsedge Street, almost directly opposite the 'Theatre

Royal', at a cost of £900. Here they held lectures and public meetings to advocate their ideas of shorter working hours, education and better conditions for the working man. The 'Owenites' were opposed by every vested interest going including employers and the church and after only a few years they were forced to sell the hall to, ironically, a church organisation for only £450. The 'Temperance Movement', who campaigned against the evils of drink, used the hall for public meetings until the late 1920's.

In 1937 the 'Oldham Playgoers' Club' decided to take over the lease of the 'Temp' as it was known, and convert it to a theatre. They purchased 217 seats from Miss Horniman's 'Gaiety Theatre' in Manchester, lay coconut matting down either side of the cold auditorium floor and white-washed the walls. As for the stage, well, it has been admitted by members since that mistakes were made, "In their amateur ignorance the officials considered that the raking of the stage was essential, and the local joiner who did the job saw to it that they certainly got what they asked for!"

Roger Williams

The committee engaged Roger Williams to bring his company to the new theatre on a long term basis and sloping stage withstanding, they decided to present a varied programme. However, things were not ready yet - the magistrates were unimpressed with the state of the

A scene from the play 'Autumn Crocus'

'Temp' and refused to grant a public theatre license. The members merely re-grouped and, on legal advice, formed the 'Oldham Repertory Theatre Club' - clubs didn't need licensing! The club now had 200 paid up members and a membership drive was launched in a bid to attract another one thousand - the idea being that you paid an annual subscription and made a donation when attending a performance.

By the end of 1937 the theatre was ready to open its doors and on Saturday January 31st 1938 they performed their first opening night with George Bernard Shaw's "Arms and the Man". As one of the founder members was to recall years later, the whole thing was a massive gamble, "On the first night we sat muffled up in the icy foyer, listening to every footstep that approached and wondered whether or not it was a potential shilling. Seats were free but we asked members to drop a shilling in the bowl."

That first performance was pronounced a great success - professional theatre had returned to Oldham! During 1938 the club

Wynn Sheridan in 'Captain Banner' in 1938

presented a whole range of productions, a new play every week with the cast performing one show at night and rehearsing another in the day. As the weeks went by so the membership numbers swelled and the club faced another, if not altogether unwelcome problem - how would they fit everyone in?

It soon became apparent that larger premises were needed if the club was to satisfy its aims and meet the increasing demand for seats. As luck would have it of course, just one street away sat the disused 'Colosseum' and the club committee eventually made enquiries about taking over the lease. After a few weeks of negotiations the lease was signed on May 23rd 1939 and the club made an immediate and important decision - to change the theatre's name to 'Coliseum'.

Much work needed to be done at the new theatre and the now 2,000 members were galvanised into action. The floor of the stalls and stage area was one large expanse of soil - wooden board flooring was laid, a proscenium arch was installed, a proper stage was built and the whole interior was given a coat of paint. The conversion back to a theatre cost £700, which was to be paid off over two years. The only thing about the building that they couldn't change was the fact that is was largely built of wood and therefore couldn't meet modern health and safety standards so denying it the chance of being granted a theatre license.

Of course, the club had experience of this problem and so continued to operate their "members only" policy to get around the law.

On July 15th 1939 the company performed for the last time at the 'Temp', it was Peter Blackmore's "Lot's Wife" and after the final curtain the cast and members sang "Auld Lang Syne". Two days later and they were opening at the 'Coliseum' with "Poison Pen"…. they never did let the grass grow under their feet!

Once again, new proprietors were taking over the 'Coliseum' and hoping to make a success of this wonderful building!

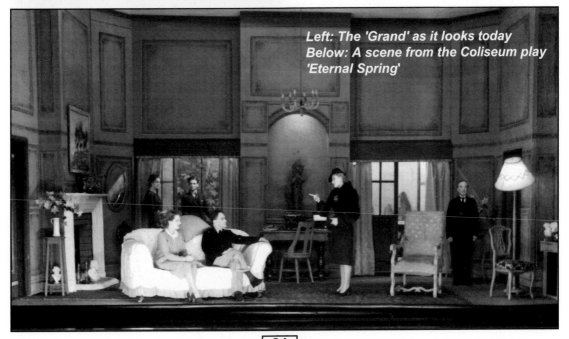

Left: The 'Grand' as it looks today
Below: A scene from the Coliseum play 'Eternal Spring'

Left: Douglas Emery at the Coliseum sound desk in the 1940s.

Below: Chris Bond doing the same job 40 years later

Chapter 5: This Happy Breed
1940 - 1949

With the outbreak of War in 1939 had come fears that Manchester would bear the brunt of enemy action and that the new theatre would be forced to close after only a few months operation. These fears were largely unfounded and indeed, during the war years under producer Douglas Emery, membership of the club continued to grow.

In 1942 a building fund was established to begin the task of raising money to pay for a new post-war theatre such was the committee's confidence. However, the forties were lean years financially and the coffers failed to swell as quickly as anticipated - for the time being, the club had no option but to stay put.

The forties proved to be a productive period and weekly 'rep' attracted a veritable who's who of new faces to Oldham including Pauline Yates, Eddie Williams, Marius Goring, Maria Charles, Beatrix Lehmann, Mollie Sugden, Joan Heath, Anna Wing, Willoughby Gray, Frederick Valk, Maurice Hansard, Violet Fairbrother, Janet Cameron, Mary Morris, Jean Forbes-Robertson and Phyllis Neilson-Terry. Several local actors were also given their first taste of fame including Eric Sykes, Dora Bryan, Lally Bowers, Alan Rothwell and Bernard Cribbins.

During the forties and fifties many actors toured the country making a living as 'guest stars', visiting one rep company after another, often playing the same role week after week with different co-stars and on different stages. No doubt these actors, who came knowing the lines and the moves, were a boon to producers who had just six days to rehearse and stage each production from scratch. During the war years many famous names including British film actors travelled the country to escape the London blitzes and Oldham attracted its fair share to make special appearances including such 'names' of the day as, Percy Marmont, Olive Sloane, Robert Newton, Milton Rosmer and Cilli Wang.

The bombing of London also meant that major companies were evacuated to the north west and used as arts ambassadors, as the Old Vic put it at the time, "...to keep arts alive in war-time and to see that they are enjoyed by people who are usually scanted of the chance for such pleasures and appreciations." One of the benefits for Oldhamers was that the Old Vic, Ballet Rambert and Sadlers Wells Opera Company all paid regular visits to the 'Coliseum'. Amongst those who appeared at this time were Sir Lewis Casson, Dame Sybil Thorndike, Donald Ross, Dame Wendy Hiller, Renee Bourne Webb, Ann Casson and John Garside.

The committee presided over the 'Coliseum' with, it is claimed, something of an iron rod. Actors had strict codes of conduct as did members and with an ever-increasing membership list, they could afford to be

A 1941 production of 'The Squall' with Dora Bryan,
Maurice Hansard and Douglas Emery

tough. The club's President was Mrs Florence Jagger, who in 1940 was aged 76, and it was part of her job to read scripts and ensure the quality of the product met the committee's strict criteria. As the membership grew and the club began allowing visiting uniformed servicemen to attend the productions, the theatre increased the number of performances so that by the middle of the decade there were eight performances weekly - Monday, Wednesday and Friday at 7pm, Tuesday, Thursday and Saturday at 6.45pm and Tuesday and Saturday matinees at 2.30pm. Extra seating was also installed and the theatre could now take over seven hundred patrons per evening. Despite all these changes still not everyone could be fitted in and it was said that when the Chronicle announced the death of a member there were usually five or six applications made for their seat before the funeral.

The increase in attendance brought with it many new theatregoers and the ever thoughtful committee lost no time in explaining the rules, *"From time to time I have mentioned various club nuisances,"* went one missive, *"...the chatterers, seat-savers etc but here is a new type which has come into existence lately - I am referring to members and friends who leave the theatre before the show is over. It generally starts with seats being banged as they stand up, then a pause for hat fixing and bag-gathering, accompanied by loud conversation. This is merely a prelude to a blundering exit and the throwing open of the rear doors. I appeal to members to have a little thought for others! Can we also ask ladies to remove their hats, we men do loathe to have to crane our heads to peer round a giant begonia!"*

The forties proved a fertile period for actors and writers however there were many instances when the choice of play had to be changed at the last minute. There were very few sets of scripts available at that time and so, companies loaned a set for the week and then sent them on to the next company planning to stage the production. Actors were barred from making notes in ink and spent the last day of rehearsals carefully rubbing out their pencil notations! All this lead to some sticky moments, as a former company member once recalled, "The film star Mary Morris came to Oldham to guest star in "Lottie Dundass" for the week. Only one set of scripts existed and they should have arrived on the Monday for the start of rehearsals. By Tuesday they had still not arrived and frantic searches were made for them. On Wednesday morning when everything seemed hopeless it was decided to attempt to do another play for Miss Morris. The missing scripts, however, came to

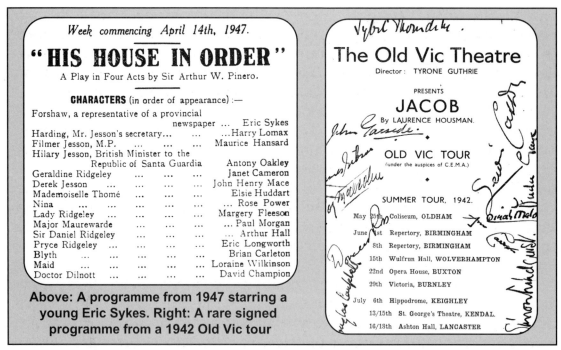

Week commencing April 14th, 1947.

"HIS HOUSE IN ORDER"

A Play in Four Acts by Sir Arthur W. Pinero.

CHARACTERS (in order of appearance):—

Forshaw, a representative of a provincial newspaper ...	Eric Sykes
Harding, Mr. Jesson's secretary... ...	...Harry Lomax
Filmer Jesson, M.P.	Maurice Hansard
Hilary Jesson, British Minister to the Republic of Santa Guardia	Antony Oakley
Geraldine Ridgeley	Janet Cameron
Derek Jesson	John Henry Mace
Mademoiselle Thomé	Elsie Huddart
Nina	... Rose Power
Lady Ridgeley	Margery Fleeson
Major Maurewarde	... Paul Morgan
Sir Daniel Ridgeley	... Arthur Hall
Pryce Ridgeley	Eric Longworth
Blyth	Brian Carleton
Maid	...Loraine Wilkinson
Doctor Dilnott	David Champion

Above: A programme from 1947 starring a young Eric Sykes. Right: A rare signed programme from a 1942 Old Vic tour

The Old Vic Theatre

Director : TYRONE GUTHRIE

PRESENTS

JACOB

By LAURENCE HOUSMAN.

OLD VIC TOUR

(under the auspices of C.E.M.A.)

SUMMER TOUR, 1942.

May 25th	Coliseum, OLDHAM	
June 1st	Repertory, BIRMINGHAM	
8th	Repertory, BIRMINGHAM	
15th	Wulfrun Hall, WOLVERHAMPTON	
22nd	Opera House, BUXTON	
29th	Victoria, BURNLEY	
July 6th	Hippodrome, KEIGHLEY	
13/15th	St. George's Theatre, KENDAL.	
16/18th	Ashton Hall, LANCASTER	

hand on Thursday and the company just got down to it....four days later we opened!"

In 1945 the war ended and the theatre tried to resume normal operations. The first problem encountered was the lack of a car park and with petrol rationing ending more and more theatregoers wanted to bring the motor. The committee purchased a piece of land at the rear of the 'Coliseum' and so, for the first time more or less, they could offer parking spaces for members. There were other changes too - part of the circle foyer was partitioned off for office space, a committee room was provided and stricter rules came in with regard to showing ones membership card...after one member was caught using a card four years out of date!

In 1946 the committee was forced to consider the future of the theatre when the lease ran out and the landlord refused a renewal. Instead, he offered to sell the theatre to the club for £15,000. Using the money in the building fund and an interest-free loan from the bank they managed to raise just over £11,000 and after some careful negotiations the landlord accepted their offer. The club was not content to stand still however, and they still harboured a desire to move somewhere a bit more modern as the newsletter of the day states, "The theatre and surrounding site are now the property of members. Miss

Phyllis Bennett and Mr Eric Landless-Turner were very proud to sign the deed giving us possession on your behalf on Friday last. Now that the building is our own we hope to make temporary improvements which will make the theatre more comfortable during the period that will elapse before we are able to build our new permanent home."

Never ones to rest on their laurels the committee decided to take productions on mini tours and so, for the first time (although the experiment would be repeated on many occasions in the future) a 'Coliseum' production played in another town - in this instance, Halifax. The scheme was short lived partly due to the fact that casts became tied up on one production for two weeks at a time and the organisational skills required for maintaining this just weren't there.

In 1947 tragedy, and notoriety, touched the theatre. The second production of the year was "Macbeth", considered so unlucky by actors that they refuse to speak the very name and refer to it simply as "the Scottish play". During one of the performances, the fight scene between Macduff and Macbeth went horribly wrong with the young actor Harold Norman, playing Macbeth, being accidentally stabbed. At first the cast were unaware of his injuries until he managed to crawl into the wings and medical assistance was summoned. Many people tell today of ladies in the audience screaming and Mr Norman dying on the stage - as dramatic as these accounts are, they simply aren't true. Harold Norman was rushed to hospital where he died some weeks later from his injuries. Over 200 people attended his funeral. It is often said that his ghost haunts the auditorium and there have been numerous sightings down the years.

Post war austerity took its toll on the 'Coliseum' later in the year when Tuesday matinees were scrapped due to problems caused by the fuel shortages, "Don't grouse if the theatre happens to be cold on the night which you attend," read a members notice, "We are advising people to bring hot water bottles and if you would like your bottle filling I think we can oblige." 1947 also marked an important event: Dame Edith Evans and Valentine Dyall performed for one night only in "Poetry and Music" which was broadcast from the 'Coliseum' on BBC radio.

1948 was another year of change, club President Florence Jagger died and the theatre was given another 'make-over' with new seating (numbers were reduced by 100 to provide extra leg-room), improved backstage accommodation and a couple of new dressing rooms. The 'Temperance Hall', which at the time was being used as a workshop and scenery store, however was looking the worse for wear and was officially declared unsafe. Sadly, as a new decade loomed, so the black clouds gathered again and the future of the 'Coliseum' was once more under threat.

The 'Temperance Hall' which had been declared unsafe is pictured under repair and (inset) Douglas Emery

Above: The auditorium of Oldham Coliseum Theatre

Right: A programme for the visit to Oldham Coliseum of Dame Edith Evans in 1947

Oldham Repertory Theatre Club
(In Association with the Arts Council of Great Britain)

PRESENTS:

THE APOLLO SOCIETY
in a Programme of

Poetry and Music

READERS:

Dame EDITH EVANS
VALENTINE DYALL

PIANIST:

ANGUS MORRISON

SUNDAY, DECEMBER 14th, 1947,
at 3-30 p.m.

PROGRAMME — 3d.

Holt, Richardson & Co., Printers, Oldham

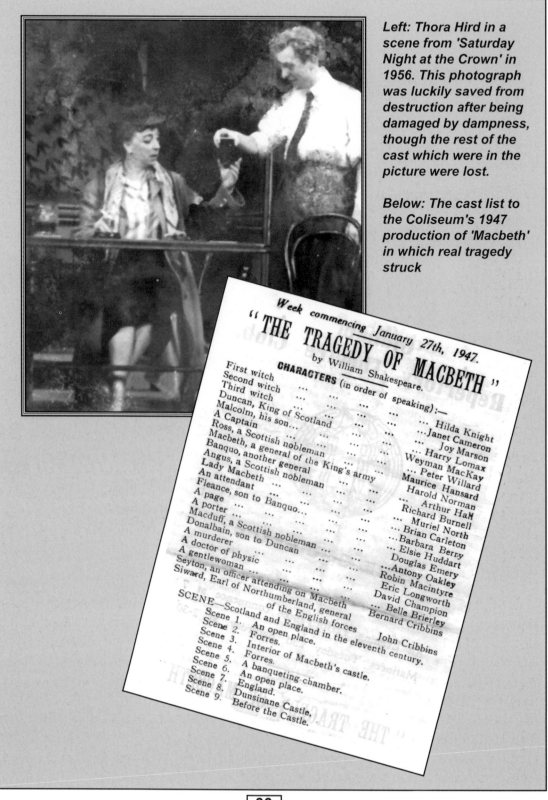

Left: Thora Hird in a scene from 'Saturday Night at the Crown' in 1956. This photograph was luckily saved from destruction after being damaged by dampness, though the rest of the cast which were in the picture were lost.

Below: The cast list to the Coliseum's 1947 production of 'Macbeth' in which real tragedy struck

Week commencing January 27th, 1947.

"THE TRAGEDY OF MACBETH"
by William Shakespeare.

CHARACTERS (in order of speaking):—

Character	Actor
First witch	Hilda Knight
Second witch	Janet Cameron
Third witch	Joy Marson
Duncan, King of Scotland	Harry Lomax
Malcolm, his son	Weyman MacKay
A Captain	Peter Willard
Ross, a Scottish nobleman	Maurice Hansard
Macbeth, a general of the King's army	Harold Norman
Banquo, another general	Arthur Hall
Angus, a Scottish nobleman	Richard Burnell
Lady Macbeth	Muriel North
An attendant	Brian Carleton
Fleance, son to Banquo	Barbara Berry
A page	Elsie Huddart
A porter	Douglas Emery
Macduff, a Scottish nobleman	Antony Oakley
Donalbain, son to Duncan	Robin Macintyre
A murderer	Eric Longworth
A doctor of physic	David Champion
A gentlewoman	Belle Brierley
Seyton, an officer attending on Macbeth	Bernard Cribbins
Siward, Earl of Northumberland, general of the English forces	John Cribbins

SCENE—Scotland and England in the eleventh century.

Scene 1. An open place.
Scene 2. Forres.
Scene 3. Interior of Macbeth's castle.
Scene 4. Forres.
Scene 5. A banqueting chamber.
Scene 6. An open place.
Scene 7. England.
Scene 8. Dunsinane Castle.
Scene 9. Before the Castle.

Chapter 6:
Hubble, bubble, toil and trouble!
1950 - 1959

If the forties had been a period of progress for the 'Oldham Playgoers' Club" then the fifties were a decade of stalemate, disagreement and bitter in fighting.

Douglas Emery who had been the Producer since 1940, and a very successful one at that, began to have serious misgivings about the future direction of the theatre. His concerns caused much debate amongst both members and committee members with the result that as the years progressed, battle lines were drawn and a bloody fight threatened to engulf the entire organisation. These problems hung over the fifties like a great black cloud.

Putting the political problems to one side, this was another period that produced a rich array of new actors and actresses including Ronald Magill, Ann Rye, Harry Towb, Keith Marsh, Nova Pilbeam, Jose Scott, Claude Hulbert, Jean Alexander, Donald Bradley, William Moore, Tony Tanner, Harold Innocent, Frank Middlemass, David Daker, Geoffrey Atkins, Robert Keegan, Anna Cropper, William Roache, William Maxwell, Henry Livings and Meg Johnson. In addition, Bernard Cribbins, Alan Rothwell, Pauline Yates, Eric Sykes and Dame Thora Hird made occasional appearances at the 'rep' and Dame Peggy Ashcroft and John Laurie made one off 'guest appearances'.

There were three other names worth mentioning at this juncture, all of whom made their first appearances at the 'Coliseum' during the late fifties and who were all destined to run the theatre in years to come - Carl Paulsen, Brian Howard and Kenneth Alan Taylor, but more of them later. One loss to the company was the actor Maurice Hansard who died in 1950 after spending nine continuous years at the 'Coliseum' playing over four hundred roles - something of a record! Members held a collection so that he might be remembered by a memorial at the theatre and indeed, still in the Circle Bar today, is a plaque to his memory.

The theatre now boasted the services of a uniformed commissionaire, the serving of coffee or oxo in your seats during the interval and an "informative and educational programme". Despite these new services and the rash of new faces on the stage, attendances decreased slightly during the early part of the decade, partly due to the public bickering of company officers and partly due, so the committee claimed at the time, to "a stream of dull and damping criticisms which we have lately been receiving from a particular press correspondent."

Mr. Cooke, Commissionaire at the Coliseum in 1950

The problem arose because it was local press policy at the time to give what were termed "non-critical" reviews of commercial theatres alongside "critiques" of 'Coliseum' productions. A bitter war of words ensued between editors and committee members with the result that the theatre made a very public appeal to, "Come and see the play yourselves.....your opinion of the play will differ very considerably from that of this correspondent!"

Towards the end of 1950 Douglas Emery announced his intention to resign his post. Within a week the committee had appointed his successor, Guy Vaesen, who had 'guest produced' on three shows during the previous year. The shock waves caused by Emery's impending departure spread far and wide and there was uproar amongst many members who felt that he had been pushed out. Such was the anti-committee feeling that a petition of 766 signatures caused there to be a Special General Meeting of all members during the pantomime season of 1950/51. The sitting committee, fearing they would be ousted, made a direct appeal for calm, "This club has been hard to build and easy to demolish," they wrote. A vote of no confidence in the committee was passed and the club's officers then decided that every member of the club should have a vote on their future before they actually threw in the towel. It was a particularly nasty period, as was recalled by the then Chairman, "The campaign against us relies on whispered rumour and innuendo which is varied according to the susceptibility of the listener; the illiterate pamphlet; the slogan chalked on the lavatory wall. This has already cost us £450 and we deprecate this unnecessary expenditure."

Guy Vaesen

A splinter group was formed under the title '*Oldham Repertory Friends' Association*' and they did indeed unseat many of the founder members - taking almost complete control of the club in August 1951. However, the problem of Douglas Emery's resignation and the appointment of Guy Vaesen was to haunt them for some time yet - Emery decided to stay, waiting for Guy Vaesen's contract to expire, however, when it did expire Emery announced that he wanted the post of Producer to be given a wider remit and be re-titled Producer-Manager. The committee was once more split, Emery resigned again and they finally let him go. In his place Yvonne Le Dain was appointed Producer and a popular member of the acting company, Harry Lomax got the job as her assistant. Within a few months Yvonne Le Dain had resigned and Harry Lomax became Director of Productions, a post he kept until 1959.

Under Guy Vaesen and then Harry Lomax, the club began to experiment with new styles of staging including being one of the first theatres to dabble with projected scenery. There was a great deal of interest generated in the national press and the club capitalised on it to boost the flagging membership figures. Just as things were looking up along came another problem - the 'Temperance Hall' which had been condemned in 1939 now needed urgent repairs and so, in the week that they staged "Dangerous

Harry Lomax

Thora Hird in a scene from the 1956 production of 'Saturday Night at the Crown'

Corner", the club committed a large chunk of the building fund to rebuild the hall. At around the same time planning permission was granted for the building of new dressing rooms, a 'Green Room', staff room and a kitchen - to help pay for it, a car parking charge was levied and members were urged to, "Please park your cars closer together!"

That was not the only interesting instruction issued to theatregoers in the fifties, we also had, "Ladies, hats do not have to have enormous upswept brims to annoy....even un-upswept ones with a solitary feather sticking up can be rather like the line on a television screen flashing before your eyes." There was also, "A suggestion that we should forbid pipe smoking and confine cigarette smoking to the intervals only."; and finally, "A word to the person who 'saw the film' and persists in keeping up a running commentary for the 'benefit' of their friend, it's always a she, about what is going to happen next. There are only a few morons loose amongst us but, they can spoil the evening for more people than they may realise."

Television had been a threat waiting to happen for many years - as early as 1944 members had been assured that, "The development of television will not be a big rival, and if the people get good theatre they will always prefer the living actor to the projected shadow." By the mid-fifties however, theatres were feeling the effects of broadcasting and in 1953 the 'Coliseum' decided that if they couldn't beat them then why not join them when they produced a stage version of the popular radio serial "The Archers". In 1954 television came a calling and the BBC arranged to make a television broadcast of a performance of "I Capture The Castle" from the 'Coliseum' stage - all went well until the local transmitter broke down and Oldhamers failed to witness the spectacle.

At the beginning of 1956 the theatre was back on something of an even keel and a scheme was hatched to re-floor and re-seat the auditorium. During this period the company would have to move out of the theatre and so, for the second time, the 'rep' took to the road for a mini-tour visiting small venues such as those in Crompton and Shaw. Whilst the actors were out of the way work was also undertaken to decorate the exterior, carpet the circle and unveil a mural in the foyer. The new look theatre was described as a "Palace".... and palatial behaviour was expected as a programme from the period explains, "I must complain about the behaviour of a small section of junior members...there is no excuse for whispering, giggling, loud repetition of lines, running about in the intervals or climbing on the seats. It is obvious that the club will be much better off without these thoughtless, ill-mannered, young people and they will be expelled from the club with a full report sent to their parents."

In December 1957 the club presented its 1,000th production, George Bernard Shaw's "Arms and the Man", the same play which had been their very first production nine years before. Amongst those who sent anniversary greetings were Sir Laurence Olivier, Dame Edith Evans, Dame Flora

A rare photograph of the Coliseum Board taken in 1957 to celebrate the 1,000th production at the theatre

Robson and Sir John Gielgud who wished the company much success.

By 1959 the club was running buses from towns like Rochdale and Halifax to bring people to the 'Coliseum' and there seemed to be something of a renaissance for theatre going. Once more however, trouble broke out amongst the club members - founder member Phyllis Bennett resigned saying she had had anxiety about the "way things are going" for some time - more of which would be revealed later. It then became known that the committee had decided not to renew Harry Lomax's contract and once more petitions called for a vote of no confidence in the committee. The committee won the day - just - and another member of the acting company, Carl Paulsen, replaced Lomax.

Carl Paulsen and George Woolley in 'Tobias and the Angel' in 1959

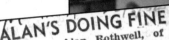
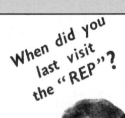

ALAN'S DOING FINE

YOUNG Alan Rothwell, of Shaw, still busy making a name for himself on stage, screen and radio (out of school hours), made a good job of his role as the cheeky boy in the programme "Under the Barber's Pole" with Wilfred Pickles on Tuesday. He has that sharp, cocky manner that goes down well with such material. Tommy Thompson's new Lancashire sketches are clever character observations.

During the day Alan is busy rehearsing at the Coliseum with the Oldham Repertory Company, for next week he is due to play three roles in the family saga, "The Golden Door," Sylvia Reagan's American play about Russian Jews in New York. Alan will be three generations of young Hynies in the Felderan family. He has one of the most touching moments in the play all to himself when he makes the coming-of-age speech at the family party.

Top left:
A membership drive in 1959.
Top: Advert for a leading lady in 1956.
Above: Christopher Guinee and Beronice Barron in 'Dead on Nine' (1956)
Far left: Janet Munro appeals to young members in 1959.
Left: A newspaper clipping from 1952 about a young Alan Rothwell

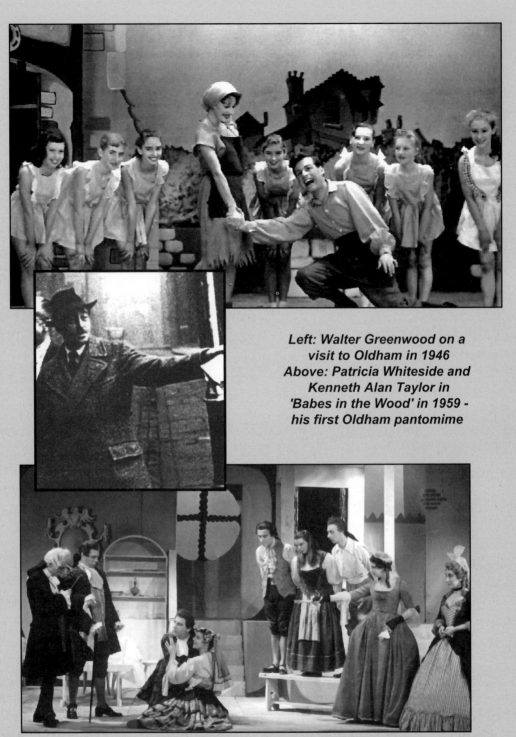

*Left: Walter Greenwood on a
visit to Oldham in 1946
Above: Patricia Whiteside and
Kenneth Alan Taylor in
'Babes in the Wood' in 1959 -
his first Oldham pantomime*

*A special production in 1954 of 'Mine Hostess' adapted by Ronald Magill, better
known as 'Amos' in TV's 'Emmerdale'. Harry Lomax is on the far left*

Chapter 7: The Paulsen Years
1960 - 1969

With the appointment of Carl Paulsen as Director of Productions in 1959, the club had got someone who cared passionately for the theatre but was unafraid of speaking his mind. He inherited what can only be described as something of a mess, membership figures had been falling by around one thousand a year, the shortfall of box office income was having to be made up by fund-raising activities and attendance figures averaged 45%. There were those who felt expansion was the answer and moves were made to acquire the disused 'Hippodrome' theatre in Rochdale (this had been on the cards for sometime and was one of the factors which contributed to Phyllis Bennett's resignation) so that plays could transfer there. In the end, it was decided to sit tight, increase ticket prices and embrace modern works and new plays.

For the first twelve months of the sixties, attendances did rise, by 7%, but controversy surrounding swearing on stage and new writing curbed any major revival in fortunes. At the end of 1961 it was decided to overhaul the company, Carl Paulsen was given a new title, Theatre Administrator and a wider remit, amalgamating his job with that of the Theatre Manager, with young actor Kenneth Alan Taylor appointed as his assistant, a post he would hold for a few years. Approaches were made to funding authorities regarding grants and, perhaps most significant of all, £20,000 worth of renovations were to be undertaken to comply with licensing requirements so that for the first time in over twenty years, the theatre might consider admitting non-members. Eventually, 'Oldham Council' and the 'Arts Council' both agreed to assist the

'Coliseum' and the passing of time saw the renovations scheme reach a £45,000 estimated cost. However, work was delayed until 1964.

The sixties saw another raft of new company members including Maryann Turner, Judy Dickinson, Ted Valentine, Ian Cullen, Ray Moore, David Killick, Shirley Stelfox, Kevin Lindsay, Barbara Knox, Colin Edwynn, Geoffrey Hayes, Richard Frost, Sheila M. Price, Giles Havergal, Judith Barker, John Savident, Frederick Pyne, Pauline Jefferson, Jane Lowe, Glyn Worsnip, John Jardine, Gareth Gwenlan, Bridget Brice, John Link, Nita Valerie, Mavis Rogerson, Knight Mantell, Freddie Lees, Roy Barraclough, Julie Goodyear, Peter Dudley, Malcolm Patton, Jean Fergusson and John Mundy. Guest stars included Jessie Matthews, Richard Murdoch, David Kossoff, McDonald Hobley, Adele Leigh, Derek Bond, Nat Gonella, Lynne Carol and Pat Phoenix.

Carl Paulsen decided that the theatre should have a higher profile in Oldham and took advantage of invitations to address various public organisations to promote his views and thus catch the headlines. Amongst his more outspoken remarks was, "One of my greatest ambitions is to have the theatre recognised as being as important to the town, as, for example, its swimming pool or library, for it serves the need of a good many residents, and with what we may call proper help, could serve more." But perhaps his most famous one was, "Apart from the Rep, Oldham is culturally very dead; I only wish the civic authorities recognised us as being as important as entertaining foreign trade delegates." His ploy worked and Paulsen became one of the highest profile bosses the 'Coliseum' has ever had.

To arrest the decline in attendees the 'Coliseum' management decided that they had to act in order to attract additional younger members and so, they expanded the entertainment on offer to include jazz evenings and art exhibitions. As Kenneth Alan Taylor said at the time, "It was suggested on television and by a youth group that someone should work on the 'mods' and 'rockers' theme in the arts. Personally I don't think this is the answer. Not every schoolboy and girl is a 'mod' or a 'rocker'. They like the Beatles, OK so do I, but they have other interests as well….(young people) have several reasons for not coming to the 'Coliseum' - they seem to think that actors and actresses are a bit odd and very different from their families. I think this image has grown up from the behaviour of some of the more sensational stars who cast off husbands and wives ad lib. and generally carry on in a sensational manner."

Technical staff continued to experiment with scenic design and effects and in the early part of the decade, tried to introduce patrons to the new technology available with special sound and light demonstrations, "We wish to show you," said one poster, "how, when playing a solo part, lighting can create atmosphere, violent theatrical effects, become a stimulant for the imagination and together with music, provide an evenings entertainment." There was also an attempt to cash in on the popularity of television by teaming up with 'Granada' to produce a season of productions as a try-out for future broadcasts, and an attempt to lure people from their TV's by the launch of a short-lived baby-sitting service. By the end of 1962 membership figures were beginning to show a slight increase however, there was still a large cash shortfall and amongst the various schemes hatched to encourage new business was the idea of issuing of 'Green Shield Stamps' with ticket purchases.

In 1963 the club celebrated its silver jubilee with a special season which included talks, jazz concerts and an anniversary production of "Salad Days". Frank Hanson, who had been Club President until 1961 wrote, "In spite of occasional and sometimes unavoidable misunderstandings, we are a happy club. But more is needed - a rededication and upsurge of the faith expressed by the pioneers will ensure our future for at least another twenty-five years." By the middle of 1963 Frank Hanson was Chairman and he could happily report that, "We have seen a remarkable recovery during the first half of the year." New confidence encouraged the committee to programme such events as opera weeks, ballet and revues, and to invite back many of the former company members who were now beginning to appear on television - it was a policy which was to pay off handsomely.

One of the side issues raised by the development in programming was the call for a banning of smoking in the auditorium. Actors would put up with it but opera singers certainly would not. In 1964 Carl Paulsen appealed to theatregoers to, "Try to confine pipe smoking to the intervals." Although he stopped short of bringing in a ban he did offer to reduce the amount of smoking on stage and indeed, in February 1964 a national attempt to legally ban smoking in theatres failed. In the same year the plans were unveiled for the renovation work which would include, a stalls bar, a lounge bar and café, an orchestra pit, a safety curtain, a sweet shop and coffee servery in the foyer - but the biggest change was that all the wooden walls had to be replaced by brick.

A large cast for a 1964 production of 'Lady Windermere's Fan'

By the middle of 1965 the new stalls bar and coffee lounge were open but the theatre was forced to close for a six week period for further work and for some months, company members were reduced to staging recitals and revue nights in the bar. It is perhaps interesting to note that these entertainments played to about 50% capacity whereas the 'sherry evening' was a sell-out! On February 22nd 1966 Lord Rhodes of Saddleworth officially re-opened the new look theatre, joining Club President Kenneth Hirst and the buglers of the "Junior Soldier's Company of the Lancashire Brigade" on stage to cut a ribbon and start a run of "The Boyfriend".

In 1967 the company embarked on another tour of sorts when it was decided to transfer all productions to the 'Theatre Royal' in Saint Helens for a few weeks. Thus, each production played for one week in Oldham and one week in Saint Helens. The experiment was deemed a success but too costly to continue on a long-term basis. The committee wrestled for some time with solutions to the problems of cost and the lack of rehearsal time - there had been a growing view that for larger productions a week's rehearsal was no longer enough. In the end, they decided that productions would run for a fortnight instead of a week thus allowing a two-week rehearsal period. This controversial news was released in July 1968 and it was also announced that the first three productions under the new system would star big names. The very first fortnightly presentation would be "Suddenly Last Summer" starring Pat Phoenix followed by "Coronation Street" star Lynne Carol in "Little Boxes" and then David Kossoff starring in his own play "Big Night For Shylock" after that. Six weeks of sure-fire box office success!

Two important changes were coming about towards the end of the decade - the change to fortnightly 'rep' and the plans to "go public" and admit non-members. Neither was wholly popular and the *Oldham*

Evening Chronicle' regularly printed letters for and against. One reader wrote of admitting the public, "The present members may be sparse but they are quiet during the performance, and nobody rips up the seats if the play doesn't come up to standard. If the public are admitted to our theatre it will be open to all the rabble of Oldham to go into out of the rain."

By the end of 1969 the 'Coliseum' had followed other 'reps' by going fortnightly however, they had taken so long over it that most other theatres were now monthly but it would be some years yet before things in Oldham changed that drastically. The issue of admitting non-members still hadn't been resolved and it was to take more time and a down turn in fortunes before that spectre would be confronted once and for all.

Far Left: A programme for 'Aladdin' in 1965
Centre top:Bridget Brice, John Jardine and Roy Barraclough in 'Richard II' in 1967

Top right: Judith Barker in 'Bus Stop' in 1960
Middle right: Carl Paulsen and Barbara Knox in 'A Shot in the Dark' (1964).
Bottom left: Barbara Knox in 'This Happy Breed' (1964)

Above: Robert Keegan and Eric McCaine in 'Simple Spymen' (1962)

David Kossoff and Kenneth Alan Taylor in 'Big Night for Shylock' in 1968

Giles Havergal and Frederick Pyne (on drums) star in a 1963 production

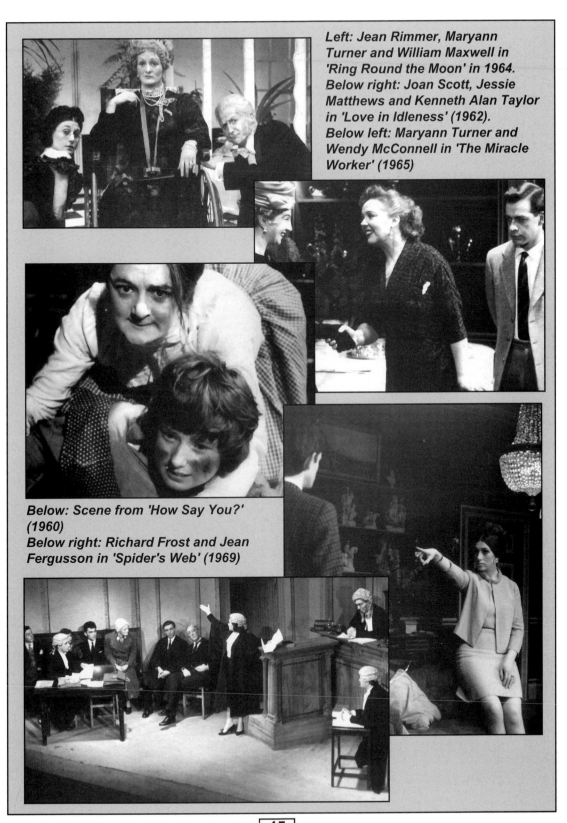

Left: Jean Rimmer, Maryann Turner and William Maxwell in 'Ring Round the Moon' in 1964.
Below right: Joan Scott, Jessie Matthews and Kenneth Alan Taylor in 'Love in Idleness' (1962).
Below left: Maryann Turner and Wendy McConnell in 'The Miracle Worker' (1965)

Below: Scene from 'How Say You?' (1960)
Below right: Richard Frost and Jean Fergusson in 'Spider's Web' (1969)

*Nicolette McKenzie, McDonald Hobley and Barbara Knox in
'Plaintiff in a Pretty Hat' in 1967*

Carl Paulsen and Barbara Knox in 'A Shot in the Dark' in 1964

Kenneth Alan Taylor, Prentis Hancock, Roy Barraclough, John Jardine and David Killick in the 1968 production 'The King's Mare'

The front cover of the Coliseum's pantomime programme for 1963

A scene from 'The Ghost Train' in 1969.
Jean Fergusson is second from the left and Roy Barraclough
standing on the far right.

Top: Scene from 'Quo Vadis' in 1965, with extras played by cleaners and staff! The young girl at the front is Anne Kirkbride, who later became famous as Deirdre in Coronation Street. Bottom right: Pauline Jefferson, John Jardine, Joan Scott and Sheila M. Price in 'Lord Arthur Saville's Crime' (1966). Bottom left: Roy Barraclough as Henry VIII in 1968.

Chapter 8: Rolling stones
1970 - 1979

The new decade began on a high - on April 22nd 1970 the theatre received its first, and only, royal visitor when Princess Margaret called in for a few hours whilst on a visit to the region. It is said to have been a pleasant, if formal, visit although had she known that Queen Victoria's coat of arms had once graced the auditorium she might have been minded to ask why it had been consigned to the skip during the refurbishments of the previous decade!

The seventies were just as rich a source of new company members and amongst those making their debut or chief appearances were Stephen Bent, Gorden Kaye, Jill Huskisson, Anne Kirkbride, Kathy Staff, David Beale, Matthew Kelly, Malcolm Bullivant, John Dryden, Karen Petrie, Alan Gaunt, Ishia Bennison, Eden Phillips, Mark Wynter, Malcolm Hebden, Paula Tilbrook, Edmund Kente, Jim Whelan, Anna Keaveney, Marlene Sidaway, Peggy Ashby, Trevor Griffiths, Alan Meadows, Sue Jenkins, Peter Hill, Ivor Danvers, David Fleeshman, Jeffrey Longmore, Michael Le Vell, Paul Oldham, David Ross, Cliff Howells, Ian Mercer and Robert Kingswell. The seventies though, was the decade of the 'special guest' and amongst those filling that niche were Oldham favourites Jessie Matthews, Dora Bryan, Alan Rothwell, Jean Alexander, Roy Barraclough, William Roache, Barbara Knox, Patricia Phoenix and Lynne Carol but also Bernard Youens, Gordon Wharmby, Bryan Mosley, Philip Lowrie, Alan Browning, Peter Adamson, Diane Keen, Bruce Trent, Dawn Addams, Mike Harding, Frank Marlborough and Kathy Jones. The growth of television was certainly having its effect on the 'Coliseum' stage!

51

The seventies began with a steady decline in ticket sales and a rise in overheads. Severe measures had to be taken - the café stopped serving teas on weekday afternoons and there was to be a hike in prices too. "For as long as it is economical tea will remain at 6d. per cup however," read one programme notice, "owing to the increased price of commodities, we are compelled to increase the price of coffee to 1/- per cup forthwith." There were also public appeals for new members and reminders that, "You can come and see a play without being a member!" Carl Paulsen faced much public criticism of his choice of plays and was forced on the defensive, "Business since Christmas has not been good," he wrote, "There were a considerable number of you who stayed away from "The Italian Girl" because you thought it was a dirty play..... and stayed away afterwards. While attendances have not increased what has increased and is still doing so, is the cost of running the theatre.......it's your theatre and it's your problem!" At that time, audience numbers were declining by approximately eighteen people each and every week..

Paulsen's frustration with his audience seemed to grow and he began making headline-hitting comments again such as, "At a recent lecture I was asked if I thought audience manners were deteriorating. Well, I don't think they are ...... oh! Of course they are, and always have been, a tiny minority of theatregoers who arrive late, who enthusiastically unwrap toffees, who come back late from the bar after the interval. I am sure that YOU don't do any of these things!"

'Cinderella' in 1975, the antics of the ponies are revealed later!

By the beginning of 1972, thanks to the generosity of the 'Arts Council' and 'Oldham Corporation' the 'Coliseum' seemed to be back on a more even footing. The council was by now giving an annual subsidy of £8,000, which caused some non-attenders to complain that other council services would suffer. Once again, Carl Paulsen put pen to paper to defend his theatre, "I read in the *Chronicle* a letter recently from a reader saying that the rep was full of snobs and there was no room for the cloth cap brigade....well that's about the biggest load of old rubbish that I have ever heard about the rep....Now I don't particularly want people sitting in the stalls with cloth caps on....nor do I want anyone sitting there with tiaras glimmering....all I want is an alert audience. Oldham is changing and some of the changes are painful but when the new town emerges we hope that its rep will be one of its outstanding features."

As that new town did emerge so the 'rep' company spread their wings. In 1973 they were invited to send a production to Kranj, Oldham's twin town in what was then Yugoslavia. It was decided that "How's The World Treating You" would play for one week in Oldham before heading east to Kranj. The production starred Sheila M. Price, Judith Barker, Karen Petrie, John Jardine and John Mundy and along with Carl Paulsen and Philip Wigley they would spread the work of the 'rep' farther than ever before. However, Carl Paulsen was taken ill and Peter Dudley took his place. The trip was a success but Carl's illness heralded a disaster that no one could have imagined at the time.

Carl Paulsen, Dora Bryan and Kenneth Alan Taylor in 'Dora at the Coliseum' in 1973

Top Left: Sheila M. Price and Terence Brook in 'Crown Matrimonial' (1975)

Top right: Andrea Koniuch and Peter Dudley in 'Two and Two Make Sex' (1975)

Bottom: The Coliseum stage is extended in 1973

On May 10th 1973 Carl Paulsen passed away, he was aged just forty-seven and had worked at the 'Coliseum' for some fourteen years. His funeral was one of the biggest Oldham has ever seen, one hundred and fifty floral tributes, hundreds of mourners - civic, theatrical, audience members and family. "He had the quality of attracting people's love," said the Vicar of Oldham, "He belonged to us in Oldham, and the vast number of people who are here this morning shows that he belonged to us in a very special way. There was clearly a force inside him, a vision driving him on." Some months earlier his photograph had appeared in the local newspaper with the following quote, "Carl Paulsen, Rep administrator, manager, producer, director, actor and the man who locks up when everybody else has gone home." Today, in the theatre foyer hangs a photo of Carl in a scene from "Charleys Aunt", beneath it is just that quote.

Michael le Vell made his first Coliseum appearance in 1978

The choice of Carl's replacement surprised many people. Victor Graham had been, for a just a few months, House Manager and he moved quickly to announce his policy, "In many ways my methods will not be Carl's, but in the most important thing of all we would not differ - in our complete and utter love of the theatre." Graham had inherited falling box office receipts and, amid the three-day week, oil crisis and high inflation, there would have to be a miracle to turn the situation round. As the club often did in the time of crisis, they decided to expand. A scheme to construct a new fly tower, stage and workshop was unveiled - the cost would exceed £40,000 and the money came largely from the 'Arts Council' and local authority. It was argued that these new facilities would enable larger productions, new technology and thereby increase attendance.

After the pantomime of 1973 the theatre closed for a short period to allow for the completion of the works. During this time Victor Graham left and a new Artistic Director, Patrick Masefield, was appointed. The grand re-opening was announced for March 1974 - "Arsenic and Old Lace" starring "Coronation Street" stars Jean Alexander, Bernard Youens, William Roache and Bryan Mosley. Such was the success of

*Meg Johnson and Malcolm Hebden in
'Rattle of a Simple Man' in 1973*

this production that the run was extended - despite only being able to use 40% of the available stage lighting due to the energy crisis. Patrick Masefield would not keep his post long however, and by the summer of '74 John Jardine was in charge with the title Director of Productions. The quick succession of chiefs tells its own sorry story.

John Jardine, had been an actor with the company since the mid-sixties and was a popular choice to run the theatre. His first few months were positively rosy, "I cannot put into words how grateful I am to you all for supporting this new season," he wrote, "So many people have spoken to me in the foyer saying, "It's like old times: the atmosphere is back!". If this is so, I am delighted, for coming to this theatre should be a happy experience." By 1976 however, finances were causing the usual struggles and the Chairman, Joan Wilkinson made an important announcement, which heralded greater involvement by the 'Metropolitan Borough Council'. This involved, the council selling tickets, paying certain salaries, assistance with theatre-in-education projects and what was described as, "a thorny problem", having council representation on the theatre board.

In June 1976 John Jardine stood down, having presided over another difficult period. He was replaced by another former rep actor Brian Howard who tried hard to keep the club above water - he brought back former company members, revived classics and premiered new writing such as one notable musical, "Clogs" which was written by one Stanley Wood - father of Victoria.

In 1977 it was becoming clear to all involved with the 'Coliseum' that things couldn't continue as they were. The council agreed to buy and maintain the theatre building and along with the 'Arts Council' and 'Greater Manchester Council' agreed to give regular financial subsidies. After all the years of letters to the press and public battles, the club died very quietly indeed. The first Artistic Director under the new regime was Kenneth Alan Taylor, once again a former company member and for some time, Carl Paulsen's number two. Taylor had the difficult job of appealing to the former 'rep' audience and those perceived as the new young, municipal audience of the future. His choice of plays was to cause delight and controversy.

Alan Gaunt, Sheila M. Price, John Dryden, Jessie Matthews and Anne Kirkbride in 'Hayfever' in 1972

Above: John Jardine, Sheila Price and Kathy Staff in 'The Corn is Green' in 1970.
Right: Kenneth Alan Taylor on his appointment as Artistic Director in 1978, and Below: A rare picture of the entire Coliseum company and staff in 1979

A scene from the 1971 production of 'Wuthering Heights'
starring husband and wife team Judith Barker and Kenneth Alan Taylor

Top: Meg Johnson, Sheila M. Price and John Dryden in 'George and Margaret' (1973)

Right: Sheila M. Price pictured in 1975 during a break from appearing in 'Crown Matrimonial'

Chapter 9: A New Spirit
1980 - 1989

By the beginning of the decade Kenneth Alan Taylor had established himself as someone willing to accept the challenge of falling revenue head on - he decided that he had to attract new audiences and widen the age appeal of the productions. In this light he began presenting new and varied works - not always successfully, not always un-controversially, but always with the goal of bringing new people to the 'Coliseum'.

By the end of 1981 he had presented ten premieres including "Fur Coat and No Knickers" which broke all box office records and subsequently embarked on a national tour, "The Rocky Horror Show", and "A Majority of One". There was also a realisation that the theatre had to embrace modern business methods and so commercial sponsors were sought for the first time and the theatre launched its own range of merchandise.

The 80's proved a hugely successful period with "One Night Stand" and "Having A Ball" both transferring into the West End and a whole string of further premieres including "Catch 22", "Spend, Spend, Spend", "Bent", "Cracks", "Whistle Down The Wind", "The Moorcock", "Time Gentlemen Please!", "Ello, Ello, Ello", "Skyhooks", "Stiff Options", "The Sighting", "The Great Eric Ackroyd Disaster", "Our Gracie", "Pennine Pleasures", "The Railway Children", "Cleanin' Windows", "Bin Woman and the Copperbolt Cowboys", "Girlfriends", "Mary Hepton's Heaven" and "Hold Tight It's Sixties Night" by authors as diverse as Mike Harding, Alan Plater and Bill Tidy.

Kenneth Alan Taylor and Sue Jenkins audition a goat for the 1980 production of 'The Hunchback of Notre Dame'

Picture by kind permission of Oldham Chronicle

It was certainly a production powerhouse that began to attract a good deal of national media attention. It was also a period which launched many notable careers and amongst those who joined the company, under different regimes, were Russell Dixon, Paul Gabriel, Lesley Nicol, Keith Ladd, Ian Bleasdale, Sheila Carter, Carole Todd, Peter Alexander, Bernard Latham, Toke Townley, Elizabeth Kelly, Sally Ann Matthews, John McArdle, Keith Clifford, Fine-Time Fontayne, Dennis Blanch, Jane Hollowood, Leonard Fenton, Rob Spendlove, Stuart Golland, Colin Meredith, Stuart Wolfenden, Wendy Jane Walker, Bob Goody, Jane Cox, Maria Friedman, Michelle Holmes, Helen Atkinson-Wood, Steve Halliwell, Tim Dantay, Mark Stratton, Janette Beverley, Veronica Doran, Jack Ellis, Tara Moran, Eric Potts, Denise Black, Charles Foster, Beverley Klein, Billy Hartman, Andrew Dunn, Philip Bretherton, Mark Chatterton, David Dale, Mike Holoway, Caroline O'Connor, Peter Straker and someone who the *Oldham Advertiser* described as, "Possibly the answer to Romeo, a new young actor...", Ralph Fiennes. Amongst those making guest appearances were Lynne Carol, Judith Barker, Sue Jenkins, Ann Rye, Bill Waddington, Malcolm Hebden, Helen Shapiro, Meg Johnson, John Jardine and Ken Dodd.

By the end of 1980 there was a new optimism about the place and for the first time in quite some years there was cash to be spent on upgrading the facilities - £10,000 was found for a new heating system, new stage curtains were purchased and a new lighting board was on order. By 1981 the 'Coliseum' was building a reputation as something of a launching pad for new drama -"We are making a modest contribution", insisted one press release - and they were picked to take part in a 'national festival of new plays' which was being run by BBC radio. Writer Alan Bleasdale was commissioned to write his comedy "Having A Ball" which then premiered at the 'Coliseum', transferred to London and on to BBC radio using the Oldham cast. It was arguably this one production which kick started the unprecedented wave of premieres that I have already listed.

Kenneth Alan Taylor was to reflect later, "I still recall with horror our Music Hall first night not long after I got this job, a blizzard outside, about twenty five brave, well wrapped, people in the audience, a cast performing the opening number in Victorian swimwear and goose pimples! Business dropped and then we took our biggest gamble, a play with a cast of fourteen, "Celebration" - it paid off and we were back in business. During "A Majority of One" we were on all three TV channels with interviews and excerpts from the play, records were broken with "Having A Ball", and then the biggest smash of all, "Fur Coat and No Knickers" - new plays were our salvation."

During this heady period a number of productions ran for extended periods -the move had already been made from fortnightly to three weekly productions, almost un-noticed back in 1979. At the end of 1981 it was announced that Taylor was to take a year long sabbatical and the former Artistic Director of Manchester's 'Contact Theatre' Caroline Smith would take over. Under Smith's control the theatre continued to make great strides including three more premieres and the return of 'local boy made good' Henry Livings. At the end of his sabbatical period Taylor made a brief return to the 'Coliseum' only to announce his departure in September 1982. "I never thought when I walked into this building in 1978 that we'd now have the reputation for being one of the most adventurous theatres in the country. So what memories will I take with me - the first night of "Bent", a play most people said could never be presented in Oldham. The result - a standing ovation on first night. Viv Nicholson in tears as she watched her life recreated on our stage in "Spend, Spend, Spend", the excitement during the run of "One Night Stand" as London managements drove up to see it and Sir John and Lady Mills coming to see "Whistle Down The Wind"....!"

Kenneth Alan Taylor left to run 'Nottingham Playhouse' and the new face at the 'Coliseum' was Pat Trueman, a former BBC drama director. One of her first acts was to experiment with pricing - for a time all seats were one price - and to try and involve more local organisations with the running of the venue by launching projects such as playwriting competitions. In 1984 money was forthcoming from 'Greater Manchester Council' to upholster the seats and with a windfall from 'Oldham Community Lottery' the auditorium was re-carpeted. There was some concern over future funding when the government announced plans to scrap Metropolitan Borough Councils and bring in a system of "voluntary co-operation" where arts organisations were of more than local importance. The 'Coliseum' joined other building based companies in pushing the government on this issue.

Paula Tilbrook with Jeffrey Longmore, Ted Morris, Ian Burns, Patrick Nyland and Paul Gabriel in 'Fur Coat and No Knickers' in 1980

Denise Black in 'The Threepenny Opera' in 1988

In the middle of 1985 Pat Trueman left and was replaced by John Retallack. Almost immediately a major refurbishment scheme was announced which was described by the 'Oldham Chronicle' thus, "The wizened brown face has been lifted, and the fresh heart beats with vigour." The exterior was painted and re-lit with the canopy light bulbs being changed from white to multi-coloured - "..for eye-catching appeal like a continental theatre..." - the foyer was opened up and the public areas were all re-decorated. The work cost £60,000.

In 1987 the theatre launched a 'Centenary Appeal' with the aim of raising £100,000 to be invested in such a way that the future could be assured. Dora Bryan carried out the official launch and descendants of Thomas Whittaker made the first donation. The public was told, "The Coliseum is not financially safe. Even a temporary financial crisis would mean the end of live theatre in Oldham."

The following year and John Retallack decided it was time to move on, blaming pressure and a job offer in his native Oxford for the decision. Paul Kerryson who was then Resident Director at the 'Library Theatre' replaced him. As he told local reporter Paul Genty at the time, "A lot of what has gone on at the Coliseum before has been worthy, I

65

love opera, particularly Puccini. I want someone to offer me the job of directing "Tosca". The emotions and the melodrama appeal. I do not know what Oldham people like but I have enough confidence in myself to try and find out."

Kerryson already had a strong reputation for his populist musicals before he reached Oldham and it was this skill for which his time at the 'Coliseum' will be most remembered - from "Chicago" to "Hot Stuff" he produced musicals which are still talked of today.

Top: Beverley Klein in 'Piaf" in 1989

Bottom: Ralph Fiennes, Stuart Golland and Chris Barnes in 'Cloud Nine' in 1986

The company of 'Me Mam Sez' in rehearsal. From left to right: Carl Forgione, Ian Marr, Ralph Fiennes, Judith Barker, Paul Slack, Diane Whitley, Malcolm Scates, Helen Atkinson-Wood, Michelle Holmes and Jeffrey Longmore in 1986

A scene from the harrowing 1980s play 'Bent'

Tim Donnelly and Michael Cashman in 'French Paste' - 1991

Chapter 10: Rollercoasters!
1990 - 1999

The nineties were a decade of extremes - largely financial - but also a decade in which the 'Coliseum' would have to face the harsh realities of surviving as a business in a more modern cut throat world.

The period began well with predictions that box office successes would allow Paul Kerryson to pay off the deficit which, on his appointment, had stood at £73,000. The then Administrator Chris Moxon confidently told reporters, "On Paul's arrival our audiences jumped and they haven't faltered since." In 1991 they had achieved their goal and the theatre was solvent for the first time in many years, however, it was accompanied by calls for a reduction in public subsidy and Kerryson would find like Carl Paulsen before him, that paying off your debts does not necessarily endear you to the funders or the public.

Despite the healthy financial state, the centenary appeal was stepped up with stars such as Alan Rothwell, Bernard Cribbins and Bill Waddington giving of their time to boost donations. By the beginning of 1991 £52,500 had been raised and the appeal, after four years, was just over half way to its target. The appeal relied heavily on past and present 'Coliseum' actors and the nineties added greatly to that list. Of those making their first or major appearances were John Bardon, Tim Flavin, Josephine Blake, Stephen Beckett, Maggie Norris, Charles West, Stephen Donald, Berwick Kaler, Minnie Driver, Neil Dudgeon, Michael Cashman, Val Lehman, Amanda Noar, Joan Turner, Nigel Pivaro, Tom

Higgins, Sarah Payne, Siobhan Finneran, Mark Charnock, Caroline Milmoe, Sheila Bernette, Eddie Kidd, Ian Kelsey, Sarah Lancashire, Steven Pinder, Ian Aspinall, Brian Croucher, Ross Boatman, Stephen Hancock, Deborah McAndrew, Gareth Thomas, Lynette McMorrough, Norman Rossington, Pepsi, Anne Charleston, Millicent Martin, Ben Hull, Ursula Smith, Patrick Mower, Sandra Maitland, Zena Walker, Roy North, Matthew Vaughan, Louise Plowright, Bill Champion, Angus Lennie and Zoë Henry. Of the guest stars, Siân Phillips, Barbara Dickson, Roy Barraclough, Paul Shane, Frederick Pyne, Lily Savage, Alan Price, Meg Johnson, Hinge and Bracket, Ian Mercer, Val Doonican, John Jardine, Kenneth Alan Taylor and Judith Barker are most notable.

Under Kerryson, now being described as "Mr Musicals", a number of shows started life including "Hot Stuff", "Hold Tight It's Sixties Night" and "Ladies Night" and there was a notable co-production with Bolton's 'Octagon' of "Teechers". The theatre was riding high and was rarely out of the pages of the local press though, once or twice it also made the nationals. In February 1991, during the Gulf War, the theatre staged "Privates On Parade" which local MP Geoffrey Dickens objected to, "It's

Picture by kind permission of Oldham Chronicle

Diane Whitley, Marie Jelliman, Linda Jane Holmes, Caroline Strong, Minnie Driver and Seamus O'Neill in 'Raving Beauties' in 1991

not the sort of thing we want on," said Mr Dickens, "It's totally insensitive. It portrays our armed services as nincompoops!" The show had been programmed well before the conflict had broken out and the theatre management refused to 'pull it' but the nationals had a field day!

In May 1991 Paul Kerryson announced he was leaving to run the 'Haymarket' in Leicester. "I'm quite happy here but I'd have been mad to turn this job down," he told reporters. He was replaced by freelance director Warren Hooper who said after his appointment, "I have always liked the Coliseum Theatre and its homely Victorian atmosphere, and I know actors enjoy playing so close to the audience. I will keep the public of Oldham entertained."

Courtesy of the Oldham Chronicle

Dora Bryan launches the Next Stage Appeal in 1991

The summer of 1991 saw a number of other changes at the 'Coliseum' including the start of described performances for the visually impaired, the launch of a corporate entertainment scheme and the computerisation of the box office. By the end of the year the financial situation seems to have taken a downturn with staff predicting that they "think we can just balance" the books. In the end, a £46,000 increase in the 'Arts Council' grant softened any problems.

At the beginning of 1992 there were plans for developing the facilities to include a bistro, rehearsal room, corporate hospitality room, refurbished dressing rooms and the conversion of the old 'Lion's Den' café into a circle bar. Dora Bryan and Nigel Pivaro launched the scheme, which would cost £300,000, and an appeal for £100,000 to put towards the costs. By September much of the work had been completed and Barbara Knox and Peter Plouviez opened the new rehearsal rooms and dressing rooms. The "French-style" bistro opened in October offering, as the *Oldham Chronicle* put it, "A smart and tasteful area...open from 11am to 11pm daily offering good food.....and an amiable little wine list."

Ian Kelsey (in white tie), now famous for his doctor's role in 'Casualty', pictured in 1993 with the cast of 'A Slice of Saturday Night'

In 1993 there was a note-worthy sighting of the theatre ghost during a performance of "Rutherford and Son" with one theatregoer telling staff he hadn't enjoyed the play though when the man with the sword had come on he'd hoped it would liven things up a bit......there was no such actor! Other people reported lights changing colour and strange shadows on the set behind the actors. Financial troubles loomed again at the close of '93 when the 'Arts Council' was rumoured to be considering ending the subsidy to the 'Coliseum'. There was the usual exchange of letters in the local press with the House Manager, David Rustidge reminding knockers that, "The Coliseum has been a starting point for many actors currently to be seen on TV. The look of satisfaction and contentment on the faces of our audiences, spending a couple of hours away from the rigours of everyday life, clearly demonstrates the theatre still has an important role to play." In the end, the 'Arts Council', perhaps minded that it was after all the "Year of Drama", awarded a reduced grant and National Heritage Secretary Peter Brooke made a visit to see a performance of "My Mad Grandad" to celebrate.

1994 was a year of headlines - Sarah Lancashire visited in order to announce plans to present studio work in the new rehearsal space, "This will be an experimental platform for dance, drama and music." she told the press. Unfortunately, the room had a tin roof and performers found it difficult to use when it was raining outside! The theatre was also used that year for the recording of a radio version of J.B. Priestley's "Lost Empires" starring Tom Baker, Freddie Davis and Bridgit Forsyth and in the June there was a stand-off with the 'Royal Exchange' over the rights to stage Ayckbourn's "Absurd Person Singular" - the 'Exchange' won. By the end of the year however, they were celebrating in Oldham with five '*Manchester Evening News Theatre Awards*' for local projects including best musical and best actress for Sarah Lancashire's role in the 'Coliseum's' "Little Shop of Horrors". There was sadness too however when founding father Joe Holroyd died aged 76.

By the middle of 1995 finances were stretched again and the non-profit making bistro was forced to close, the Daily Telegraph noting that.."This is arguably the last working class theatre in Britain. There's nothing to eat but pork scratchings and Maltesers but the bar is still recommended for its gritty lack of pretension." There was also an interesting gaff that year - GMR's Jimmy Wagg and Eamon O'Neal were booked for a one night gig but the season brochure advertised that "GMTV's Eamonn Holmes" would be there instead - there were red faces all round!

1996 started with the theatre board and Warren Hooper in dispute and worries over what was described by the Chairman as, "The parlous state of affairs". A number of steps were taken to dig the theatre out of the crisis - the

Siân Phillips in the title role of 'Marlene' in 1996

Roy Barraclough as brother and sister Leslie and Maureen in the 1998 production of 'A Different Way Home'

board decided to impose an, arguably more populist, season of plays on Hooper, the theatre's Administrator who travelled to Westminster to appeal for increased funding, and it was announced that the £73,000 raised by the centenary appeal had been used temporarily to reduce the deficit. By February, amid predictions that Oldham would get a new theatre in a proposed 'cultural quarter', there was speculation of job losses but denials that the theatre was facing closure. In March it was announced that the post of Artistic Director was being scrapped and Warren Hooper would be made redundant with a new position of Chief Executive being created.

By the beginning of August the new incumbent was posing for press photographs in the sunshine - Kenneth Alan Taylor was back in charge for the second time. Asked what he would be giving Oldhamers he replied, "I'm going to give them what they want to see...I want them to know that whatever they come to see it's once again going to be something they will remember and enjoy." In October the final change was made when the number of board members was reduced from twenty to twelve.

Taylor was as good as his word reviving classics such as "Saturday Night at The Crown" and "Wait Until Dark", reinstating the traditional squeaky-clean pantomimes and premiering new works such as "Dead Funny", "Rebecca" and a series of home-grown musicals. A few productions caused particular interest - the new musical of "Alfie" hit the headlines when the costly production was supported by a £20,000 donation from a mystery woman; the premiere of the new musical "Marlene" starring Sian Phillips which went on to West End and Broadway success; the premiere of the Jimmie Chinn play "A Different Way Home" which won copious awards and provided a theatrical first in that actor Roy Barraclough played 'straight' a brother and sister.

By the end of the decade, and the century, the 'Coliseum' was riding high again - average attendances were at 77% and a whole run of successes smashed box office record after box office record. In ten years the theatre had gone from paying off its deficit to running one up again to just about paying it off again......a rollercoaster ride indeed.

Right: Meg Johnson and Judith Barker in the revival of 'Saturday Night at the Crown'.

Below: Kenneth Alan Taylor (right) greets Arts Minister Chris Smith who visited the Coliseum in 1999

Right: A poster for 'Mother Goose', the record breaking 1999-2000 production

Below: Judith Barker and Alan Rothwell in the 1999 production of 'Roughyeds', which celebrated Oldham's 150th birthday.

OLDHAM
Coliseum
THEATRE

FAIRBOTTOM STREET OLDHAM OL1 3SW

"I cannot imagine I'll find a better pantomime this season"
Bolton Evening News

"A blaze of colour which holds your, and more importantly your children's, attention throughout!"
Oldham Evening Chronicle

"The Coliseum is at the top of the tree"
Manchester Evening News

4 December 1999 - 22 January 2000

mother goose

Written and directed by Kenneth Alan Taylor
A cracking eggstravaganza!

Come and marvel at the Millennium Dame!
booking information (0161) 624 2829

A scene from Stephen Sondheim's 'Company'
at Oldham Coliseum Theatre in 1990

Rosie Rowell and Joan Turner in 'The Killing of Sister George' in 1992

Paul Gabriel and Jo-Anne Knowles in the 1998 production of 'Dick Whittington'

Chapter 11: Into the Future.
2000 -

For the purposes of this book we end the 'Coliseum' story at 1999 - what the next century holds we will have to wait and see. The first season of the new millennium however, included two premieres, a classic farce, a modern comedy, a thriller receiving a regional premiere and the tail end of a record-breaking panto season - surely, what regional repertory theatres like the 'Coliseum' are all about.

Two things have stood out whilst researching this history - the staggering number of actors, singers, dancers, directors, writers and technical staff who have been given their first taste of the business at the 'Coliseum' and the never-ending loyalty of its staff, particularly the voluntary staff who, for over sixty years have kept the theatre open rain or shine, financially secure or not. I started the book by saying that the 'Coliseum' was about people, not bricks and mortar - how true that is.

Oh, and by the way, in May 2000 it was announced that the deficit had been paid off. Now where have we heard that before.........?

The new Millennium got off to a fine start with a brilliant production of 'The Mysterious Mr. Love', starring Paul Opacic

Memories
and
Recollections

Dora Bryan

During the war, when male actors were scarce, I was playing Jane in "Jane Eyre" at the rep. Playing opposite me was a Rochester who was much too old and doddery for my sixteen-year-old Jane. I remember that when Rochester proposed to me an old lady in the audience shouted out, "Don't Dora love - he's far too old for you!"

I have so many happy, happy memories of the 'Coliseum' which was after all, my training ground for the future years.

I have a special affection for Oldham and its repertory theatre. Three plays of mine were premiered here; "Saturday Night At The Crown" and "Happy Days" both starred Thora Hird, and "So Brief The Spring" with Robert Newton who, on our way to the theatre one foggy night was stopped in his tracks by the, to him, fascinating spectacle of a line of young Oldham lads in clogs and all holding up burning torches made of loosely rolled newspapers. Every few steps they all, simultaneously, struck their clog-irons on the pavement to throw up a shower of fast-fading sparks.

"Did you see that?" Robert said, charmed. I explained that the lads were 'sparking'. Enraptured, he said "What a scene for a film!" Playing with him was a young student named Dora Broadbent whose performance, in the small part she had, instantly told me that here, unmistakably, was 'star' material. Later, when casting the film of "The Cure For Love" which I'd written for Robert Donat, I mentioned Dora. She was given the part and nearly stole the film.

Thora's two shows were given splendid receptions. Oldham, to me, is the most Lancashire of Lancashire towns where I always feel 'at home'.

WALTER GREENWOOD in 1973

Jack Tinker

Agatha Christie's "And Then There Were None" was a play which changed my life. In fact it was the first play I ever saw and I came home in such a thrall of terror and hypertension I could not wait to return to the 'Oldham Rep' as soon as pocket money permitted. As I was only eight at the time and the effect of video nasties and violence on formative minds was totally unknown, it was perhaps more than fortunate that my taste was tempered by the following week's offering, which was "Peg O' My Heart". Suffice it to say that I was hooked on theatre forever more!

It was at the 'Coliseum' that I was given my first chance to be a professional actor.......full of the arrogance of youth and with a pocketful of demob money, I wasn't really particular whether they took me or not. At that time I was determined to be a stand-up visual comic but fortunately for me they gave me a chance. Had they not done so I would have had to have gone into the cotton mills!

ERIC SYKES
Speaking in 1987

Steve Halliwell

I suppose my fondest memory of my time at the 'Coliseum' was playing Bottom in the centenary production of "A Midsummer Nights Dream" back in 1987. It was a great production directed by John Retallack. It's a wonderful theatre that has done well to survive the changes from cinemas to bingo halls. I have a deep affection for that little house of dreams.

Steve Halliwell pictured as 'Zak Dingle' in the popular TV soap 'Emmerdale'

Charlie Chaplin

My boyhood finished at the age of seven, for a little after that time I was busily working on the music halls, not for much it must be admitted, but I was in. At that time I was one of the "Eight Lancashire Lads". My work on that tour was arduous in the extreme; young as I was, I was an adept at dancing and acrobatics. It was excellent training for film-work, for I learned many little tricks on the dusty stages.

CHARLIE CHAPLIN
In his autobiography

I played as a guest star in many reputable reps all over England, and can honestly say that Oldham tops my list. I do hope it goes from strength to strength.

JESSIE MATTHEWS
In 1963

I was a visitor to Oldham during the war, in a production of "Guilty". I remember the warmth of the audience, and the great kindness of its patrons who housed us so comfortably in those hard days when hotels were not available to actors.

DAME FLORA ROBSON
In 1963

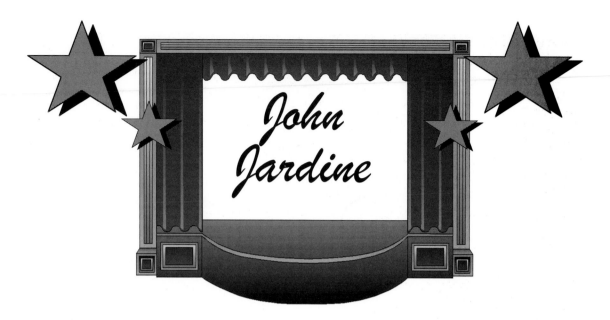

John Jardine

Of all the memories from my days associated with the 'Coliseum' I remember those when Carl Paulsen was in charge, the most. Carl had to have everything just so, he supervised everything - from props to posters - and if it didn't suit him, you soon knew about it. I remember being on stage during a rehearsal and he called the props girl to the front of the stage. She was stood there holding a tray full of props and he said to her, "I will not have props of such poor quality on my stage" and he pushed the tray up into the air so that everything smashed onto the stage. What he didn't know at the time was that they were all things he'd lent us from his own house!

I remember doing pantomime at the Coliseum - "Cinderella" it was, and Paula Tilbrook and I were the Ugly Sisters. We had a team of real ponies to pull the coach, which was bedecked in tinsel and looked rather lovely. During the night they escaped from their stables and attacked this coach, eating all the tinsel! From then on, every time they did their business - usually on stage - it always glittered!

Siân
Phillips

I have a huge soft spot for the 'Coliseum' particularly as they mounted the production of "Marlene" there, very much an unknown quantity in 1996 although it subsequently toured all over the place for four years! Playing at the 'Coliseum' was as rewarding as playing the West End, Africa and America; I loved my time there. The wardrobe ladies were fearless as they chopped and nipped and tucked costumes that had cost a fortune to make! The show was re-written every day but stage management took the mayhem in its stride. Mark Jonathan from the 'National' added light cue to light cue until the plot almost equalled Marlene's. The follow spot operator had absurd demands made on him and yet his arms never wavered. People who had worked with 'Marlene' saw the show in Oldham and couldn't believe the technical achievement.

My very favourite moment every night was watching the front of house people coming in to watch "Where Have All The Flowers Gone". My brightest memory is of the fire alarm going off after the show one night - I, confused and in my dressing gown, stood in the doorway of my dressing room saying, "Where's the exit?". No answer. Bedlam. Then the wardrobe department rushing past saying, "Where's the dress?....save the dress!" Priorities .... it warms my heart to remember!

Oldham Coliseum! - those two words must bring back so many memories to so many actors who have in their time appeared at this famous theatre. It was known to myself long before I had even seen it, never mind having appeared there.

Oldham Coliseum was to me, in line with the foremost repertory theatres in the country - the 'Citizens' in Glasgow, the 'Abbey' and 'Gate' theatres in Dublin, Joan Littlewood's 'Stratford East' and earlier of course, Miss Horniman's company in Manchester.

When I did get to see it I was appearing at the 'Windmill Theatre' in London and in the middle of a two year run, it was 1958 and I had landed a part in an "Armchair Theatre" play called "The Mortimer Touch" for 'ABC Television' at Didsbury. The 'Windmill' gave me time off to do it and I realised I would be near Oldham so I decided to go there just to have a look at the theatre. I journeyed all the way there on public transport, tram I think!, - a long way! I found the theatre and just stood there and looked at it, don't ask me who was appearing there I don't know, to me they were all so grand and far above me even though I was appearing in the West End. You see, at the time, I was hardly an actor - I was a variety and revue artist. I had been in a couple of touring plays and this TV part was a big break. So there I stood, I remember I heaved a sigh and thought, "Well, they wouldn't want me!"

In 1998 Kenneth Alan Taylor asked me if I would like to play Charlie Naughton in "Underneath The Arches" at the Coliseum. Once again I travelled north to Oldham - my former "Crossroads" mates Kathy Staff and Lynette McMorrough came to prop me up - Kenneth and I were so polite to each other (we laugh about that now!). I got the part and I had the time of my life!! It was a wonderful company and a great example of what ensemble playing should be all about. On the last night I wept, I have never done that in a theatre before and had to be consoled in the dressing room by Charles Foster who played my partner Jimmy Gold.

Well there we are, that was my time at Oldham and when you think of it, it was worth waiting forty years to get inside!

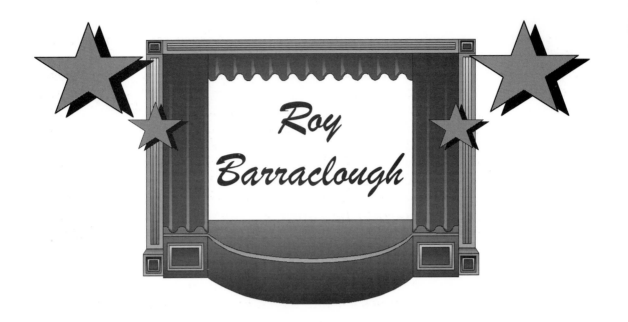

Roy Barraclough

I first joined the 'rep' company in 1966 after stints at Huddersfield and Stoke. During my years in Oldham I got the chance to play many varied roles - classics, comedies, my first pantomime dame...and to direct. It was weekly rep in those days of course and we worked damned hard for about fifteen pounds a week. You were in the theatre from nine in the morning until eleven at night, six days a week, with the same people week in, week out - it was very much a family with all the mix of tension, rows, laughter and happiness you would expect.

It's perhaps hard for people who did not work under the rep system to fully appreciate what it was like but you can imagine how stressful learning a script and rehearsing every day whilst appearing in a different show at night, could be. Saturday matinees became legendary - you were on a bit of a high by then because you had the dress rehearsal in the morning for the following weeks play and you were closing at night in the current play so there was a feeling of elation in the air which tended to go to our heads. Added to this was the fact that we had to have lunch in the café with the public who, in typical Oldham style, told you exactly what they had thought of your performance the previous week. All this caused many on-stage practical jokes during the matinees, there are so many stories....in "Anastasia", at the end of the play, after everyone realises she has gone missing from the palace I had to come down a very impressive staircase and give this long speech about what had happened - well, I just looked at the assembled 'court' and announced, "She's done a bunk!" and walked off - in fact we all walked off, completely hysterical! I also remember coming to see the company in "Murder on the Nile" and going back stage during the interval to see them - the set was the saloon lounge of this cruise ship and there were lots and lots of cane chairs. As I was going back to the auditorium for act two I remarked to Barbara Knox that I had placed a whoopee cushion on one of the chairs - none of them would sit down for the whole of the act, the audience must have thought they were mad!

Apart from the fun we had I also remember the absurdity of having to supply many of your own costumes - it was stated in our contracts that we had to have so many lounge suits plus a dinner suit. If you were lucky, as I was, then your landlady would scout round jumble sales for you looking for new outfits. There was also the fact that we had to play all ages, not like today, so people like me, John Jardine and Kenneth Alan Taylor constantly played character roles so you used to have to keep trying to get hold of different wigs and moustaches - I used to experiment with make-up and make warts and things out of latex glue! You also got to play roles way beyond you - I played Willy Loman in "Death of a Salesman" when I was in my thirties! - during the matinee I was on stage by myself giving this long, long soliloquy, and thinking I was being rather good, when I heard a single voice in the darkness of the stalls say, "Well I prefer it when they're all on, don't you Enid?".

After I left the permanent company I went back a few times during the 70's to guest star and then again in 1998 with "A Different Way Home", after a gap of twenty-two years - that brought back so many memories. These days people talk about artistic policies - there were none in our time, you got a list of plays Carl had chosen (often even he didn't know what they were about until the scripts arrived, he just liked the titles!) and a cast list and you were told who you were playing - you had no choice in the matter. That's why we got the range of experience we did - there's nothing like that now and it's criminal because there was no training like it. The 'Coliseum' was unique - it was presided over by amateurs employing professionals, for a start - and it has a unique place in the hearts of all of us who started our careers there.

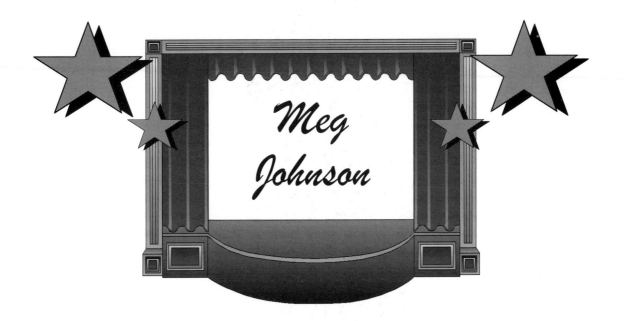

Meg
Johnson

I have always enjoyed appearing at the 'Coliseum' and there are so many lovely stories and memories but one of my favourites happened whilst I was still in the nursing home having given birth to my son Nicholas. I received a phone call from Carl Paulsen asking me to come and appear in a play called "Thin As Air" which I agreed to, terrified at the thought of telling the nursing sister that I was returning to work - and planning to take my baby with me! When I finally plucked up courage to tell her she couldn't have been more enthusiastic, "He'll come to no harm there!" she said.

So off we both went, back to the 'rep', where Carl was kind enough to move us into his dressing room, which was on the ground floor and nearer the stage. In those days you rehearsed on stage and Nicholas had this cot with wheels so any actor not appearing in that particular scene took turns to push him back and forth on the edge of the stage. I remember Giles Havergal asking, "Are you feeding him personally?" and when feeding time did come round Carl used to stop the rehearsals and off Nicholas and I would go. At lunchtimes the company used to go across the road to the 'Kings Café' which was quite posh - ladies wore hats in there - and the old ladies always looked in shock as I carried Nicholas round on my waist. You didn't go back to work so soon in those days, certainly not taking your baby with you!

Once the play opened my mum would come in every night and baby-sit in the dressing room - everyone was so lovely about it and he turned out to be a successful, well-adjusted lad so it can't have done him any harm!

Jean Fergusson

Having spent two wonderful years at the 'Coliseum' from 1968 to 1970 it is difficult to pick out just a few memories but one or two do stick in my mind.

Richard Frost and myself were delighted to have the chance to do a production of N.F. Simpson's "A Resounding Tinkle". It was a rather bizarre play to

say the least, with references to having an elephant at the bottom of the garden called Mr Trench and scathing remarks about the woman next door only having a snake which she kept in a pencil box. We thought it was hysterically funny, and although it was difficult to learn, we got through the first performance feeling very proud of ourselves. However, it was not the sort of play that the audiences were used to and at the curtain call there was a mixed response and a certain amount of bewilderment. There was this long pause and a man in the audience shouted out, "Call that a tinkle? - it were more like a bloody clanger!".

I also recall a production of "Black Comedy". The whole play relies on the fact that at the opening the stage is in darkness and the audience hear two people talking as if it were lit. Suddenly all the lights come on and the two characters say there's been a power cut. Consequently the rest of the play, although the audience can see the actors, is supposed to be in darkness. The dialogue in this opening scene is vital for the audience to understand this reverse situation. On the opening night when there was total darkness for this opening scene, the audience did not hear a word as a regular theatregoer started shouting, "Lights! Give us some lights!" and set off a chain reaction. They were suddenly all shouting, stamping their feet and lighting matches! When the lights did come up they had no idea what the plot was and most of them probably watched the whole play thinking we were blind!

I will always remember how vital it was not to be late for rehearsals and this was drummed into us from day one. Well, as everyone knows, Oldham winters can be very bad and I remember that in 1969, I had digs with the wonderful Mrs Bibby in Springhead (£5 a week inclusive of a meal after the show, breakfast if you made it yourself and Sunday lunch with all the trimmings!). I woke up one morning to find two feet snowdrifts and I had to dig my way out of the front door. There was no bus service so I walked, or rather fell, all the way into Oldham panicking all the way that I'd be sacked for being late. On arrival at the theatre, by which time it was getting on for lunchtime, I found it to be locked and deserted - I was the only one who'd got there! I apologise if this sounds self-congratulatory but it really was the fear of being late that drove me to it!

I would just add that I wouldn't change one memory of my two years at Oldham, working with a marvellous company, and I learned more about my craft in that period that I ever did before or have done since. Thank you!

Previous page: Jean Fergusson as herself and above as one of TV's most popular characters 'Marina' in BBC TV's 'Last of the Summer Wine'. Jean has also played Gary Mallet's (Ian Mercer) mum in 'Coronation Street'

Kathy Staff as her most memorable and lovable character
Nora Batty in BBC TV's popular series 'Last of the Summer Wine'

Kathy Staff

I thought I'd really made it in showbusiness when I appeared at 'Oldham Coliseum' for the first time. I had joined the acting club they had there when I was 16 and I always wanted to appear on stage in one of their plays, and I finally made it in August 1970 when I appeared in "In Celebration". I have done four plays there now, "The Corn Is Green" in September 1970 in which I played Mrs Watty, "Friends and Neighbours" in November 1970 and the last one I did, "Hanky Park" in 1973.

It was a great thrill to appear at the 'Coliseum'. I think it's a lovely little theatre, very warm and friendly, and it was such a happy place to work - it feels like belonging to a family really. When I started out I always looked up to the 'Coliseum' as the place to act and I really did feel that to perform there meant you had made it! And I must say that when I did eventually appear in my first play there, I felt it was something really special. My husband John and I still go there as often as we can to watch the plays....it's a very important theatre to me.

Kathy Staff as herself

Geoffrey
Hayes

I joined the 'rep' in February 1962 as Assistant Stage Manager/Actor, replacing the late, great broadcaster Ray Moore (who, of course, was unknown then, beyond Fairbottom Street). I had been working in an office by day and in the evenings I'd been involved in amateur dramatics in Stockport and Manchester dreaming of becoming a professional actor. Now here I was, at Oldham - my dreams becoming a reality!

This may sound odd, but my most abiding memory of my first week was the fact that everyone referred to each other by their Christian names! I was 19, had been brought up in a working environment, where one referred to our elders and betters as Mr or Miss. But here, from leading lady to humble ASM, Christian names were the order of the day!

I made my acting debut as "Gentleman Caller" in "The Glass Menagerie" on 30th April 1962. The Artistic Director was Carl Paulsen. Although charming, he did have

a temper and one was never quite sure what mood he was going to be in. I think I was a bit scared of him. He was strict and would often be found checking that stage management were going about their business and not skiving. He'd have us tidying up the prop room sometimes even after the evening show! Despite this we did manage to sneak off on the odd afternoon to the 'Kings Cinema' across the road!

Over all, my memory of my year or so at Oldham rep is one of excitement and happiness, learning my trade. It was a tough schedule, although it didn't seem so at the time, and I often left my home in Cheadle at 7am returning around midnight - all for £5 a week! I was young, keen and eager to learn and I wouldn't have missed it for the world!

Dame Thora Hird

I certainly remember my time at 'Oldham Coliseum', particularly when I appeared in Walter Greenwood's "Saturday Night at the Crown". I enjoyed it tremendously. They were a great audience to play to, being northerners they have a great sense of humour, and it was a nice, intimate theatre to play in, and "Saturday Night at the Crown" was a very funny play to perform in.

It was also a lucky play for me to appear in, for on the third night at the 'Coliseum' during the first interval there was a knock at the dressing room door, and Kathleen Williams, who was then one of the heads of selectors for an entertainment venue in Blackpool, popped her head in and said, "I hear you're at Blackpool for the season, because we're buying it!"

I remember I stayed at a hotel in Oldham called 'The Grapes', and the owners had a grown-up daughter called Alice. There was a big, open market I remember, with three massive stalls, one sold china cups, one of saucers and one of plates, and if you spent all day you could get a saucer to match a cup. Alice had a wonderful collection and down in my country place today I have about six of her cups and saucers so I think of her many times - and of my time in Oldham.

I remember they had a Singing Room at 'The Grapes' and in the play at the Coliseum, which was set in a pub's snug, I referred to the Singing Room several times. Well, one night Kathleen Williams, Walter Greenwood and myself just stood at the door of the Singing Room in 'The Grapes' where there was a man singing "Only a Rose I Give You" from "The Vagabond King" when the chairman stopped him singing and he said, "Shut up everyone! Ladies and gentlemen, there's someone who's stood at the door that we all love and she's at the 'Coliseum' this week and I hope you're all going, may I introduce Jeanette Scott's mother!"

My daughter was a child star then, you know, and we all had a good laugh about it. I'm sad to say that I've never managed to get back to Oldham. I enjoyed my time there and I'll always remember the friendliness of the 'Coliseum'.

103

Keith Marsh

Little did I think when I joined the 'rep' in 1949 that I was to be a member of that company for the next seven years.......but that is what happened! Looking back, fifty years later, those years were some of the happiest of my life. Memories of productions, actors and actresses abound - enough to fill a book. However, the lasting and most outstanding memory is of the enormous range of plays our wonderful audiences sat through in those days. They took everything in their stride from Shakespeare, Shaw, Ibsen, Coward, Rattigan, Fry, Anouilh and of course, the Lancashire farces. At that time, I think the company was unique......what other weekly rep was giving its audiences such a remarkable selection of plays, and where else could one be stopped in the street by a play-goer and told that the Moliere play last week was super! Yes, Moliere was 'box office' in Oldham in the fifties!!

Actors and actresses came and went in that period and some stayed for several years....one recalls Bernard Cribbins, John Barrie, Harry Lomax, Ronald Magill, Joan Heath, Pauline Yates, Madeleine Newbury, Janet Munroe and many, many more.

On the mantelpiece at home I have a Staffordshire china figure which appeared on many mantelpieces, in many productions and which I took with me as a souvenir when I left Oldham. I've only got to look at it and the 'Coliseum' is immediately conjured up! I feel sorry for the young actors of today, for when they come to look back after fifty years in the 'business', they won't have experienced anything like the wonderful but hardworking life we actors of the fifties had at Oldham rep!

William Roache

After a stint at Nottingham I sent out several letters to established repertory companies. One of them brought an invitation from Oldham Rep to audition for juvenile lead. Oldham, although a weekly rep, operated twelve months a year, and it also had an excellent reputation. Among actors, who tend to be a superstitious lot, it was considered a lucky place.

Brian Blessed, who had been to Bristol Old Vic drama school, helped me prepare for my audition. He worked very hard on me and his contribution was extremely positive. So when I got the Oldham job, at eight pounds a week, it was partly thanks to Brian.

I recall many productions there such as "Death and Brown Windsor", which was like a bad Agatha Christie. It was an awful play. It was all plot, times, dates and red herrings, and dreadful to learn. The play started with Henry Livings and me sitting on a sofa having a conversation. But in the opening scene we found ourselves going straight into the end of the play. Ad-libbing madly, we tried to get back. Henry fed me a line. I couldn't *pick it up. I tried a line. He couldn't pick it up. Because this play was all plot you couldn't just chat your way through it the way you could in other things! So we sat there looking out front, sweat breaking out on our fore-heads, facing the audience and totally lost. I shouted for the prompter and a plaintive voice from the prompt corner said, "You jumped and I tried to follow you and I lost the place." Everybody fell about. Then the prompter came on stage and we all studied the script. The audience were laughing, which was always good because it means they're with you. We finally got it going again and it was all okay.*

There was the annual pantomime too of course. "Robin Hood" was chosen the year I was at Oldham. Robin Hood is usually played by a principal boy, but Carl Paulsen cast me, because I was quite slim and good-looking in those days. So there I was in Lincoln green, with the tights, boots and hat with a feather in it. We had a chorus of little girls, taken from a local drama school, and the panto began with them dressed as singing pixies. Then a horn sounded and they cried, "It's Robin! It's Robin!" as I came heroically down a staircase, centre stage. On the opening night all went well until my entrance. I appeared at the head of the stairs. I threw my arms back in greeting. The orchestra swelled. Then I tripped and bumped down the staircase on my bot-tom!

William Roache went on to become one of Britain's most famous TV faces

WILLIAM PATRICK ROACHE
Born: April 25, 1932, in Ilkeston, Derbyshire

Married his present wife Sara in 1977 (three children by this marriage) Previously married to actress Anna Cropper (two children by this marriage), they were divorced in 1974.

Started studying medicine before joining the army for a stint of National Service during which time he decided to stay in the forces and became a captain in the Royal Welsh Fusiliers. He stayed in the army for five years, serving in outposts of the British Empire in such diverse spots as British Guiana (now Guyana), Jamaica and Bermuda, as well as Germany and Oman.

Turned to acting after leaving the army and appeared on TV in series such as 'Knight Errant', 'Skyport' and 'Biggles', when he was was selected for the part of Ken Barlow in 'Coronation Street', a role he has held since the very first episode in December 1960!

Jean
Alexander

In 1951 I wrote to Guy Vaesen, whom I had worked with some years earlier, asking if there was any chance of working with him again. But it was half way through the season, his company was complete, and all he could offer me was a job as wardrobe mistress and an occasional part when he could fit me in.

The day I arrived in Oldham was unseasonably hot and I had to walk from the station to the theatre carrying all my worldly possessions in two heavy suitcases. The stage manager gave me an address where I might find a room and I heaved myself and my cases halfway across Oldham. "Come in love," said the five-foot tall elderly lady with red cheeks and white hair, "As this is my daughter's house I'll have to charge you 25 shillings a week. But I'll throw in a pint of milk a day."

There was a door at the top of the stairs which she squeezed herself through. "Now this is your kitchen and bathroom," she said, indicating a rickety old table on which stood a galvanised metal food safe, black with age. Across the room was what must have been the oldest gas stove out of a museum, blue and mottled and encrusted with the remains of a thousand meals. I discovered later that only one of the rings worked. When I applied a match the flame would shoot up about 18 inches then subside to less than half an inch. One day I went to open the oven door, lifted the latch and the whole door fell off and landed on my foot - there were no pins in the hinges. Neither were there any shelves, burners nor bottom on it.

My job as wardrobe mistress was very time-consuming. We seemed to do a lot of costume plays, the clothes for which were hired from a theatrical costumiers in Manchester, and of course they had to be altered to fit the contours of the actors. The costumes would arrive on Saturday and I took the alteration measurements when and how I could on that day. On Sunday I went to the theatre to get the work done...a prospect that filled me with some foreboding, because it meant that I would be alone in the theatre for hours, and I hated the thought. An empty theatre backstage is always spooky.

On one occasion, I opened a huge skip which contained oddments and plunged my hands in to take out an armful of bits and pieces. Out jumped a rat, a huge gingery creature that landed on the floor with a thud and crouched there, looking at me. Eventually the rat, tired of the view, began to run about. He leapt on to one of the dressing tables and nibbled at a stick of greasepaint!

After four months, I decided I was not getting enough acting experience and I left, with no hard feelings between Guy and me.

Matthew Kelly

I appeared in two productions at the 'Coliseum'. In September 1971 I made my Oldham debut playing 'Cowboy' in the musical "The Boys in the Band". The cast included Peter Dudley, Carl Paulsen and Kenneth Alan Taylor who played 'Harold'. The story centres on a birthday party at which almost all the guests are homosexual and the production was considered a bit controversial at the time - I remember the Chronicle publishing a still from the show in which I was in Kenneth Alan Taylor's arms with the caption, "This is Harold and this is his birthday present!". It was a wonderful production and as I recall, got very good notices.

My second appearance came in July 1972 when I was cast as 'Elmer' in "Hot and Cold in All Rooms" with John Jardine, Sheila Price, Alan Gaunt, Peter Dudley and Carl Paulsen. All I remember of it was that I was diabolical! Oh, and there was a young sixteen-year-old girl in the cast who was the most talented actress I had ever seen. Her name?...Anne Kirkbride!

Alan
Rothwell

Ask anybody except an Oldhamer where Bernard Cribbins comes from and they will be most likely to say, "London, somewhere". Their evidence would seem incontrovertible - songs like "The Hole in the Ground", "Right, Said Fred" and many "Carry On" movies all feature Bernard and his impeccable Cockney accent. But us from up 'ere know the truth. He was born an Owdhamer as we say, and he got his first acting experience at the rep. I don't know how long he had been an actor before I met him but we first worked together on a play called "Now Barabbas-" in May 1949. He played Convict 4288 Smith and I played 'Erb, a young snotty nosed oik visiting my father (3762 Brown, played by Harry Lomax) in Pentonville Prison. My very tiny part consisted of standing around adenoidally with my mouth open until the crucial moment when I had to drop a sweet onto the floor. While the 'screw' on duty bent down to pick it up my mother slipped 3762 Brown a smuggled packet of Woodies.

Bernard and I didn't meet on stage in this play but we did meet off. He was a keep-fit fanatic and would do a pretty thorough workout as a warm-up before the show. I was quite small for my age in those days and Bernard latched onto an ingenious means for improving his pectoral and upper arm muscles. He would make me lie on the floor of his dressing room, grab me by the seat of the pants and also by the scruff of my neck and hoist me over his head as if I was a set of weights. Half a dozen press-ups later and he was ready for the performance.

Looking back at the programme for that play and I notice that it says the cigarettes were "By Abdulla". It always said that in the programmes back then and yet I cannot remember any occasion when that was actually true. It certainly wasn't for "Now Barrabas-". Cigarettes were quite definitely by John Willie Woodbine. I know because I pinched one and smoked it! Perhaps that's why I was so small for my age!

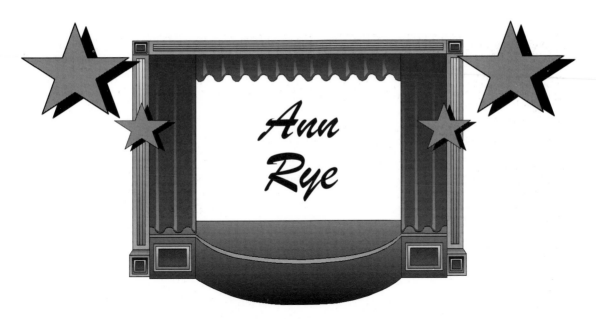

Ann Rye

Back in the days of weekly rep there were two elderly sisters who religiously came to every Thursday matinee. They approached me in the street one day and said that they were milliners and that they had a small hat shop in Oldham - on George Street I think. Anyway, they wondered if I could find a use for some of their hats. In those days actors provided all their own stage clothes so naturally I accepted their offer and said I would be most grateful.

Soon after, a box-load of hats arrived for me at the stage door, one or two of which were perfect for my next stage role. I was to play 'Pearl Cunningham' in an Australian play called "Summer of the Seventeenth Doll" which was considered a tiny bit daring at that time, which was 1958. The story centres on a group of tough sugar-cane cutters who have their girlfriends to stay every summer. At one point in the play I had to say, "I think I'll wear my little black hat" and I produced one of the hats given to me by the two ladies. No sooner had I placed the hat on my head then I heard the loud clunking of auditorium seats and I could just make out this group of women standing up and making their way out. As they reached the centre aisle they stopped and in a rather loud affronted voice one said, "...fancy that Ann Rye wearing a hat just like mine. They told me it was an exclusive!"

There can't be many people who have walked out of a show because of a hat!

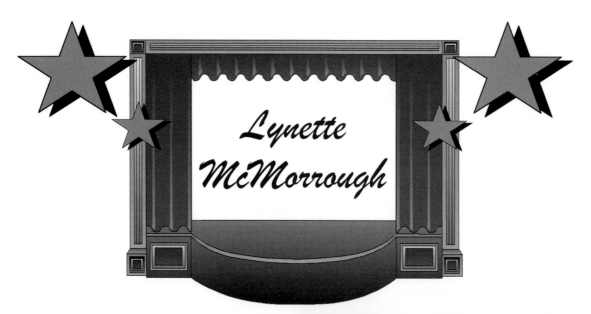

Lynette McMorrough

I have played in many theatres up and down the country over the years but the 'Coliseum' is my favourite. Sadly, two years ago, I lost my father. He too, had travelled up and down the country, collecting me at the stage door on a Saturday night, never complaining.

One of my fondest memories of my father - and the 'Coliseum' - is coming down the stairs into the foyer after a matinee to see him, having arrived early to see the evening show, sitting in the box office, with a small bunch of freesias in his hand, wrapped in soggy brown paper.

Sadly, a few years later he passed away, very suddenly and unexpectedly. Six weeks later and I started rehearsals for the 60's musical "Dancin' In The Street". I was surrounded by love and laughter at a time when I thought I'd never do either again and, on opening night; my father was there. Not with the soggy freesias this time, but he was there.

Mark Wynter

The 'Coliseum' provided me with a series of firsts in my transition from pop singer to actor. For starters, it was my first repertory theatre work and Carl Paulsen guided me brilliantly. "Five Finger Exercise" kicked off my initial visit with Anne Kirkbride playing my sister......I confess to developing more than a brotherly crush on Anne!

"Never Too Late" immediately followed which was an American play, giving me my first accented and comedic role. Then some years later I returned to appear in a play of my choosing - "A Voyage Round My Father" with Kenneth Alan Taylor in the title role, me as his son, relaying and reflecting on our life together. In the mid-seventies I was beckoned again, with an irresistible invitation, the title role in my first Shakespearean drama - "Macbeth". No disasters took place, as can often happen in a production of this gory piece, but I do recall that the actress playing Lady Macbeth had a penchant for drinking Guinness straight from the bottle during rehearsal - which clouded the Green Room somewhat! However, it didn't upset her performance, and certainly gave credence to my opening line of, "So foul and fair a day I have not seen." I worked with some outstanding actors at the 'Coliseum'. Apart from those already mentioned, John Jardine and Peter Dudley are two amongst many who were helpful in providing a springboard of excellence and a lasting foundation for my life of theatre. For me the 'Coliseum' will never be "just a memory".

Paula Tilbrook has long been associated with the Coliseum, but she has become famous in recent years playing the gossipy, but soft-hearted Betty Eagleton in the long running TV series 'Emmerdale'

Paula Tilbrook

It was January 1976, we were doing panto of course - "Cinderella" - and John Jardine and I were playing the two ugly sisters and sharing a dressing room....don't ask why, that's another story! To say that Johnnie was feeling harassed would be the understatement of the century because he was in the show, directing the show, in charge of the admin. and running the whole theatre! Now, when Johnnie is harassed he doesn't always see the funny side of things so I used to try and cheer him up, not always successfully. So intent was he on the success of the show that he used to stand in the wings at every performance during the transformation scene (when the pumpkin turns into the coach and the mice become ponies) to make sure all was well. No, this was not a pretty sight because, to make himself more comfortable for the few minutes he was off stage, Johnnie used to take off his dress and stand there in full make-up and wig, size ten heels - and his underpants - completely oblivious.

Every night, like clockwork, the two ponies that pulled Cinderella's coach would walk down the centre of the stage and cr*p!! This used to enrage John and he would hop up and down, steam almost coming from his ears. This, of course, used to make me laugh - which didn't help matters. After the transformation scene Johnnie and I had to make our entrance in front of the palace corridor cloth as if we were on our way to the ball. At every performance there, right in front of us, was this big pile of pony poo which Johnnie would frantically try to kick into the wings with his high heels. I'm afraid this used to make me laugh even more!

One afternoon, before a matinee performance, there was a knock on the dressing room door, and there stood the stage manager, "Mr Jardine," he stammered bleakly, "we have a problem - I'm afraid the ponies have broken out of their stable and they've eaten all the tinsel and fairy lights off the coach!" John went ballistic. The stage manager tried to calm him, "We can get the coach back to normal for this evening but it's going to have a little less sparkle than usual this afternoon." Johnnie realised there was nothing else he could do and the matinee went ahead.

That evening John took up his customary position to watch the transformation scene and fumed even more when the ponies left their calling card centre stage. We made our entrance along the corridor cloth and just as he was about to kick the offending pile into the wings with his size tens we noticed it was glistening in the lights, "Oh look," I whispered, "it's coming out glittered!" Johnnie's face lit up into a grin and we both fell about.....ah, happy days!

Kenneth
Alan Taylor

I arrived in Oldham on a wet winter's night in 1959. I had been brought up in London's East End but I was still shocked at how Oldham looked then - black rain ran down the cobbled streets, gas lights flickered in the gloom. But it was the Oldham people who were a revelation to me - their warmth, their humour and their blunt honesty. As audiences they laugh like no other, they respond, they enthuse and they never hesitate to tell you, "That were bloody awful Kenneth!". I met my wife at the 'Coliseum', my children virtually grew up in the theatre and I've lost count of how many times I've left only to return.....this building draws me back like a magnet.

When I started here we used to have hanging cards which announced the next six plays - we didn't have posters like today - so every six weeks you had to find six new play titles - as a result we did a real variety of work. At Easter you had to do a religious piece which was the only way you were allowed to open on Good Friday so we would tackle works like "The Robe" or "Quo Vadis" and once we got very posh and did "Son of Man".

You never quite knew what you would be doing next, I remember Carl Paulsen telling me about this play we were to do in which he wanted me to play a crippled ex-actor. I was only twenty-two so I thought it sounded marvellous to be in a wheelchair and old and crippled. When the script arrived, I read it and discovered that it was about a Welsh circus owner who discovers the second coming of Christ! Carl had mixed up the titles and we had listed it on the hanging cards so we had to do it - I finished up playing a seventy-year-old who only spoke in Welsh!

I think everybody thinks that the productions were tat because it was weekly rep but there was some amazing work done, particularly from a design point of view. Carl had high standards; he was a stickler throughout the whole theatre. He was probably the best teacher one could have. If you worked in stage management and you borrowed something for a prop and it got broken you had to pay for it out of your wages. The other thing I remember was that if you had meals on stage you would never get proper food - if you had to eat egg and chips they always put half a peach on some mashed potato to make it look like the egg! There was a lot of food in plays in those days.

I remember the first time I met Dora Bryan, she was by then a big star and I was a rep actor, she said, "My happiest time in my whole career was at Oldham Rep." I thought, oh that's rubbish, you're doing "Hello Dolly" at Drury Lane or whatever, they can't have been the happiest times. But I actually know now what she meant. We went through the same process of being part of the theatre and part of the town. It was one big family.

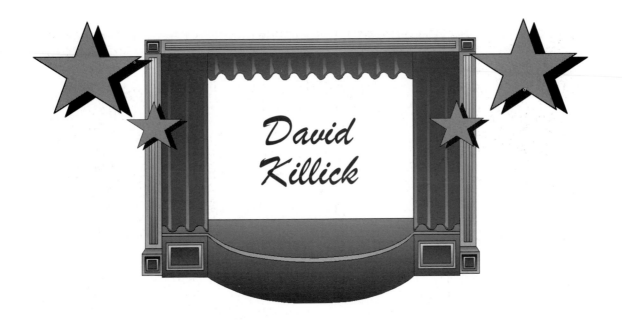

David Killick

It was early August 1966 that I took the train (steam engine!) to Oldham Mumps Station and walked up to Fairbottom Street for my first sight of the 'Coliseum'. I was really very excited, this being my first real stint at weekly repertory. I had been engaged to play the part of the Rev. Alexander Mill in George Bernard Shaw's "Candida". My first shock was being told that I was in fact to be playing Marchbanks, a large and very famous role, and the second shock was that we opened in a week's time!

Carl Paulsen, the Administrator at the time, was a very fine Director and he was so encouraging and supportive that I knew I was in safe hands, and indeed, during my time at the rep I learned a great deal from him. We really did work hard, learning an act a night whilst acting in the current play, but we managed to play hard as well - ah!, those youthful days! Being a Londoner it was a new experience for me to live in the North and I had a great time. I was looked after so well by Mrs Bibby, the best digs I've ever had and all for £2 10 shillings a week! The audiences were always very supportive, but they also let you know if they hadn't enjoyed the performance.

Wonderful characters worked at the theatre; Annie Beaumont in the Box Office who told me that my newly acquired wicker skip would look fine in my room covered with some "cretin"!; Barbara Mullaney (Knox) who was in my first play "Candida" with me; Roy Barraclough with whom I appeared in "The Odd Couple", one of my happiest times!

My time at the 'Coliseum' was both exciting and exhausting and very, very instructive in all aspects of life in the theatre and I send love to all who knew me - even if I did have to change my name from Courtland to Killick!

Eric Longworth

Eric Longworth

I am privileged to say that I began my career with the Oldham Rep at the tender age of twenty-eight - Assistant Stage Manager (ASM) playing small roles as cast, £3 per week. A slight change from Staff Captain, 'Q' Movements, Indian Army. At last fulfilling a boyhood dream, which had been re-activated whilst stationed in Bombay during 1944 when I was asked to appear with the 'Bombay Light Opera Society' and 'Bombay Players'.

It was whilst home on leave in 1945 that I made contact with Douglas Emery and told him of my previous experience as an enthusiastic amateur at school and with 'Crompton Stage Society' and to cut a long story short, twelve months later at the end of July 1946 my career began. By Christmas I had appeared in ten plays, two of which we took to Halifax and Huddersfield as part of the Arts Council's 'West Riding Tour', taken part in a poetry reading night and rounded off the year by playing a Chinese Policeman alongside Arthur Hall in "Aladdin". Bernard Cribbins played the front legs of the horse and Dora Bryan was Princess Baldroubaldour!

A year later I enjoyed being the prettier sister, Minnie Mumm to Maurice Hansard's Maxie Mumm (get it?) in "Cinderella". Dora played the title role, Mollie Sugden was Prince Charming but Bernard had gone off to Palestine to do his military service. At the end of January 1947 we celebrated the club's ninth anniversary with a production of "Macbeth" which has the reputation of being an unlucky play - nothing prepared us however, for Harold Norman's death as recounted elsewhere in this book - he died leaving a widow and a baby boy. We still had seven performances to fulfil so Arthur Hall, then an ASM, had to go on in the title role with only one night and one morning to prepare - and he did it without a prompt! Arthur had been playing Banquo so we all had to change roles, David Champion went from playing the Doctor to playing Banquo and I stepped up from Murderer to Doctor - one whole scene, thirty-three lines in fifteen speeches. Fifty years on I can still recall the fear that gripped me as I struggled to learn those lines, made worse when I realised that I had to enter 'down stage right' and stay there - as far away as you can be from the prompter who is the other side of the stage! There was only one thing I could do - persuade a fellow ASM, Brian Carlton, to stand in the wings as near to me as he could with a script in his hands - just in case! Yea verily and gad zooks....it was alright in the end! I was associated with 572 productions at the rep, starting with "The Sign on the Door" by Channing Pollock, the club's 429th production in 1946, and ending with "Aladdin" at the end of 1957. Oh happy days!

Patricia White

Carl Paulsen started life working in a shoe shop in North Shields, but got his chance when a repertory theatre was built in the Plaza at Tynemouth. He joined the company and quickly became a leading man, before going on to become Producer. I got to know him because I was the accompanist to two local singers who were often used as extras and they recommended me to the original Producer, Douglas Emery - who by strange co-incidence had come from Oldham. So, I got to know Carl and wherever he was, if he needed a pianist, he roped me in.

When he began planning his first Oldham pantomime in 1959, I got this panic phone call, "They've offered me someone with a string of letters after her name - but if you come, I know I can just say I want robber music and you'll play robber music!" After such flattery, how could I refuse!

I had to attend a ball at University the night before I was due in Oldham so I boarded the night train to Manchester wearing a long black evening gown, with trousers underneath for extra warmth. I was met off the train by Carl who was speechless with laughter at my get-up. We had to go straight to the theatre, so I had no time to change until I got there and my arrival caused quite a stir!

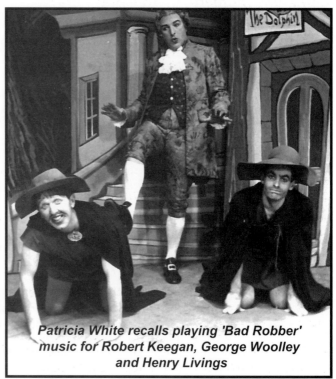

Patricia White recalls playing 'Bad Robber' music for Robert Keegan, George Woolley and Henry Livings

126

Sometime in the early 1970's Carl Paulsen was directing and playing the lead in "The Seventh Veil", a psychological drama. He was a severe Svengali-style uncle, whose niece Francesca was played by Anne Kirkbride. Francesca is required to be an expert pianist, and there is a climactic moment in the play (and in the film in which James Mason utters the immortal line to Ann Todd, "If you won't play for me Francesca, you'll never play for anyone again", slamming the piano lid down on her fingers). Talented though she was and is, Anne did not play the piano. There was a dummy piano on stage and a real piano immediately behind the scenery. A young, talented but somewhat wayward music student had been employed to play 'for' her,

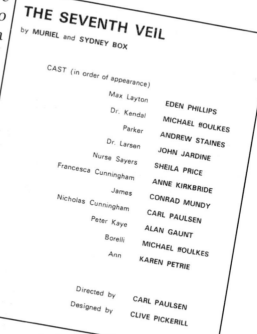

THE SEVENTH VEIL
by MURIEL and SYDNEY BOX

CAST (in order of appearance)

Max Layton	EDEN PHILLIPS
Dr. Kendal	MICHAEL ffOULKES
Parker	ANDREW STAINES
Dr. Larsen	JOHN JARDINE
Nurse Sayers	SHEILA PRICE
Francesca Cunningham	ANNE KIRKBRIDE
James	CONRAD MUNDY
Nicholas Cunningham	CARL PAULSEN
Peter Kaye	ALAN GAUNT
Borelli	MICHAEL ffOULKES
Ann	KAREN PETRIE

Directed by	CARL PAULSEN
Designed by	CLIVE PICKERILL

his cue being the activating of a green light by Anne pressing middle C. On more than one occasion the student was to be found chatting in the wings while Anne/Francesca stabbed impotently at middle C, the on-stage piano emitting nothing more than clicks and crashes.

Autographs